ANN ARBOR

BEER

A HOPPY HISTORY OF
TREE TOWN BREWING

DAVID BARDALLIS

FOREWORD BY RENE AND MATT GREFF

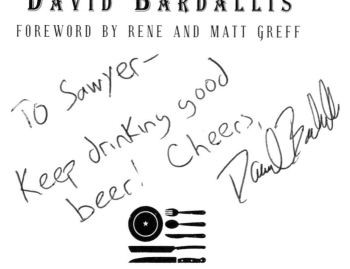

To Sawyer—
Keep drinking good beer! Cheers,
David Bardallis

AMERICAN PALATE

Published by American Palate
A Division of The History Press
Charleston, SC 29403
www.historypress.net

Copyright © 2013 by David Bardallis
All rights reserved

Cover photos by Allen Williams.

First published 2013

Manufactured in the United States

ISBN 978.1.62619.156.3

Library of Congress CIP data applied for.

*For Mom and Dad, who always knew I'd write a book
but probably expected something different.*

For my brother Mike, whom I largely blame for my beer obsession.

*And for all the local bar and brewery folks, who work hard
mostly for the love of it—cheers to you.*

CONTENTS

FOREWORD

If you've ever bellied up to the bar and tipped back a pint at a local brewery, then you know there's something special about drinking a brew right from the source. And it's more than simply quality and freshness. There's a satisfying sense of interconnectedness—a sort of Old World charm—that comes from running into your local brewer around the neighborhood or having him or her step out of the brewery to shake your hand and ask you what you're drinking. Somehow the beer just tastes better when you know the people who brewed it.

Like most Americans over forty, we grew up drinking faceless, mass-produced beer that was completely disconnected from the men who made it. We first discovered fresh, local beer and pubs in Europe during separate study-abroad semesters in college and then, later, together on our honeymoon in 1991. Matt started homebrewing in 1992 and quickly found that he enjoyed making beer a lot more than working as a database analyst. By 1993, the Michigan legislature cleared the way for brewpubs to open, and we began dreaming of our own brewery.

When we opened the Arbor Brewing Company in downtown Ann Arbor in the summer of 1995, we never could have imagined what lay in store for our brewery or our nascent industry. At the time, we were the only brewpub in Washtenaw County, and one of only 10 craft breweries in Michigan. Fast-forward to 2013, and we find ourselves gloriously awash in craft beer, with 125 breweries in operation across the state—11 right here in our own backyard!

As pioneers in a dynamic, rapidly changing industry, we've had the opportunity to play our small part in the history of brewing in Ann Arbor. In addition to being the first brewpub in Washtenaw, we were also the state's first solar brewery, the first to produce barrel-aged sour beers and the first brewpub to open a packaging brewery, and in 2012, we became the first American craft brewery on the Asian subcontinent with the opening of our Arbor Brewing Company India location in Bangalore.

Even as our industry has evolved and grown over the past decades, there are some constants that predate the post-1980s craft renaissance and stretch into the past to pre-prohibition America, as well as even farther back to our distant ancestors from faraway lands. Local breweries have always been about connections—between pub staff and customers, brewers and beer lovers and patrons whiling away the hours celebrating, mourning, telling stories and plotting revolutions large and small.

So, like any great historical tale, the history of brewing in Ann Arbor needs to be much more than mere dates, facts and figures. This story can be told only by someone who is both beer lover and drinker, journalist and historian, philosopher and social critic. There's no one better equipped for the job than Dave Bardallis, who combines a passion for the truth with the heart of a hometown boy—and an insatiable thirst for local beer.

We're proud to say that we knew Dave before he was "the Ann Arbor beer guy," although neither of us can remember exactly when we first met him. He's one of those people who just seemed like he'd always been a regular. Then, at some point, we slipped across the blurry line into friendship without any of us really noticing it (blurry lines can be an occupational hazard). Given our shared love of the flavors, history and tradition of beer; our hometown; and lively debate, our friendship was probably inevitable.

Anyone who has had the pleasure of reading Dave's beer writing can attest to his sense of humor, his gift for storytelling and his tell-it-like-it-is approach to reporting. But those of us in the industry who have had the opportunity to work with Dave can also attest to his honesty and integrity. He is simply a man who loves to drink and write and learn, and his humble and open approach to covering the craft beer business has made him one of the most well-known and widely respected craft beer correspondents in Michigan.

So, know that you are in good hands as you embark on this fascinating journey of discovery into a local history of brewing that crosses its own blurry lines into music, politics, poetry, science, medicine and even the paranormal. Pull up a pint and enjoy the ride!

Rene and Matt Greff, Founders and Owners
Arbor Brewing Company
Corner Brewery
Arbor Brewing Company India

ACKNOWLEDGEMENTS

E very author will tell you that writing a book requires the help of many other people, and this book was no exception. I'd like first and foremost to thank everyone who took the time to share stories, photographs, breweriana, memorabilia and beers with me. You are legion, you know who you are and I really couldn't have done it without you.

Special thanks are in order to two people who answered my frantic calls for assistance and gave generously of their time and talent. Allen Williams, whose beautiful photography graces these pages, stepped in on ridiculously short notice to take some amazing shots without which this book would be much poorer. And Cindy Hegenauer compiled the information for the book's appendix and helped with the index. To you both: May your beer glasses be ever full.

Many thanks are due also to the following:

To Rene and Matt Greff, for writing the foreword; for doing so much to spread the love (and the supply) of good beer around Ann Arbor, Ypsilanti and beyond; and for generally being awesome people.

To E.T. Crowe and Jessica Warth, for invaluable early advice and encouragement.

To Wystan Stevens, who may know more about Ann Arbor's historical persons and places than any other single human being alive today and was kind enough to unfailingly answer all of my annoying questions.

To Doug Smith, who shared his knowledge of, and relics from, the old Northern Brewery, and Norm Richert, who did the same for the old Michigan Union/Ann Arbor Brewing Company building.

Acknowledgements

To *Ann Arbor Observer* editor John Hilton, for letting me invade his office to rifle through many boxes of old photographs and being so good-natured about it.

To Peter Yates, for generously allowing me to reprint a number of his photos from years gone by.

To Kelly Frick of mlive.com, for doing the same with all the *Ann Arbor News* photos you see.

To Nicole Rupersburg, for sharing her picture-taking skills along with plenty of beers and listening to me complain.

To Sean Bachman, whose amazing collection helped me fill in a gap. I hope one day you find a permanent location to house that magnificent Michigan beer bottle museum.

To the staffs at the Bentley Historical Library and the Ann Arbor District Library, especially the Bentley's Karen Jania and Malgosia Myc and the AADL's Amy Cantu. You were not only extremely helpful but also super easy to work with, a quality that deadline-crazed writers appreciate very much.

To Grace Shackman, whose decades of writing on local history made my difficult task much easier.

To Greg Dooley and Mark Bomia, for sending me the awesome story about Neil Snow.

To annarbor.com, for giving me a platform to tout our great local beer scene for the past several years, and to everyone who has ever stopped me to say they like what I'm doing.

To Joe Gartrell, formerly of The History Press, whose idea this book was, and Will McKay, who helped me shepherd it through to the end.

To my family and friends, whom I completely neglected for weeks at a time to focus on this project. Thanks for understanding, and I hope you think the finished product was worth it.

And to Sam and Max, two of the coolest cats ever, who even sometimes refrained from sitting on the keyboard while their human was trying to work.

INTRODUCTION

As funny as it is to think about now, my love for the city of Ann Arbor predates my love of beer. The year was 1989, or maybe 1990, and I was one of four pimply Detroit-area teenagers, not long out of high school, day-tripping to that mecca of all that was interesting and hip on our way to a summer weekend in Irish Hills. One of us was looking for some rare import, so we stopped at the old Tower Records on South University, then Borders Books & Music, then a smorgasbord of other funky Ann Arbor locations like Wazoo Records and the Dawn Treader Book Shop. The specific memories fade.

However, the overall experience stayed with me. Whether it was the quaint nineteenth-century architecture, the tree-lined neighborhood streets, the groovy sidewalk cafés, the lively yet laidback vibe or some combination thereof, this boy from the 'burbs was hooked on Tree Town's charms.

In later years as a student, I would repeatedly get to enjoy the unique experience that is a fall football Saturday in Ann Arbor. Trips to Ashley's to try beers from around the world were always a must and helped widen my newly legal consumer's perspective. Still later, while in town, I could partake of fresh beer from these newfangled joints known as brewpubs. (Not only were these places nigh unheard of elsewhere in Michigan, Ann Arbor was so cool it had *two* of them.)

By the time I moved here in 2004, I had already become a bona fide beer dork, on a never-ending quest to try delicious new brews. How marvelously lucky for people like me that the local beer scene has experienced such incredible growth this past decade, with new breweries and beer bars steadily popping up, older establishments trading in more and more of their bland macro-brew taps for the flavorful offerings of craft brewers and restaurants of all stripes trying out the suddenly hot trend of "beer dinners."

You will read about all of those things in these pages. But what of Ann Arbor's bygone brewing era? It turns out there is some big beer history in this little town. This should come as no surprise, considering the heavy German influence that Ann Arbor has enjoyed going back almost to its founding and which is still apparent wherever you look today. For a brief period in the nineteenth century, Tree Town—then a considerably smaller place than it is today—boasted as many as six breweries operating simultaneously.

But it should be noted that this book is not intended to be an exhaustive historical record full of footnotes and esoteric details. Rather, it's designed to provide a few hours of easy reading over some pints at the pub. It tells the beer-related stories of poets, professors, prohibitionists, performers and the many others who have in some way colored Ann Arbor's past, as well as of the personalities of today who are shaping the city's present and future.

I've enjoyed having the opportunity to combine two things I love—Ann Arbor and beer—into one book, and I hope you enjoy the results of my efforts, preferably with a good brew at your elbow.

Part 1

LOOKING BACK

CHAPTER 1
JUGS OF WHISKEY, GALLONS OF BEER

S omething in the Virginian's earnest bearing reassured Elisha Rumsey that their combined efforts indeed would bring the fortune each sought and desired. Through January's bitter chill, wheresoever they called in Detroit city, the merchants and officials with whom they spoke were encouraging of the notion of the two speculators purchasing adjacent parcels here in the Michigan Territory for purposes of starting a village.

Thus it was decided that he and this spirited, younger partner of his, John Allen, would push west in the cold of dawn to discover the most advantageous location for their endeavor within the unsettled county of Washtenaw. For tonight, it was only to mark their partnership—Yankee and southerner—with the customary warmth of whiskey and ale in this hotel, where many in the barroom seemed still to prefer the rum, wine and brandy of the city's earlier French days.

Ere long, he would withdraw to his room and attend to Mary Ann, his wife, whose advanced pregnancy meant she would remain here. Allen's wife, Ann, had not yet come from Virginia. It was just as well, for tomorrow's journey under any conditions would be difficult; the heavy falling snow would only add to the discomfort.

Another tankard and then to repair upstairs. "Here now," he said to his companion, "a toast and a wish for Providence to smile upon tomorrow's undertaking. May God see fit to reward our labors with wealth and felicity!"

From its very inception in 1824, Ann Arbor has been a drinking town. The first building ever erected on the adjoining plots of city founders Elisha Walker Rumsey and John Allen was a tavern, or at least it eventually became one. Known as the "Washtenaw Coffee House," the log cabin that stood at what is now the southwest corner of Huron and First Streets was where Rumsey lived with his wife, Mary Ann, and lodged and entertained prospective residents.

"Annarbour"—as Rumsey and Allen called the claim they registered in Detroit on May 25—was officially on the map. But beer was not the main beverage these pioneers and early speculators imbibed to take the edge off those miserable days and nights filled with hard labor, harsh weather, familial squabbles, bouts of illness and generally rustic living conditions. Any brewing at this time would have been a strictly household affair, much like cooking and baking, and there are no ready records to document Ann Arbor's frontier kitchen beer. There is, however, plenty of evidence to show that spirits, particularly whiskey, were an important part of Tree Town's earliest days.

In fact, whiskey and other spirits seem to have been the preferred choice throughout the young republic. Historian Daniel Okrent noted that Americans in the 1820s were guzzling booze at a never-equaled-before-or-since annual rate of seven gallons per capita, or more than a bottle and a half of hard liquor per week for every man, woman and child. (Today's consumption is estimated to be one-third of that.)

The written histories of Washtenaw County contain numerous references to whiskey, and although this is a book about beer, a brief discursion on the early settlers' fondness for "the little brown jug" is useful background for understanding the later clashes between beer drinkers and anti-alcohol "temperance" crusaders.

According to Samuel Beakes's 1906 history of Washtenaw County, the home of one Erastus Priest served as the venue for Washtenaw's first-ever court session, which assembled in Ann Arbor on January 15, 1827, for the purpose of approving "the application of Nathan Thomas, John Allen and Jason Cross, for license to retail 'strong or spirituous liquors.'" Beakes noted that this was not only "the first business transacted" but also the entirety of the court's proceedings for the day. An earlier county history, published in 1881 by Charles C. Chapman & Company of Chicago, noted that other

An early Washtenaw County drinking establishment, the W.H.L. Roberts Tavern operated near what is now West Michigan Avenue and Carpenter Road in Pittsfield Township. Roberts eventually became a prohibitionist. *Sam Sturgis Collection, Bentley Historical Library, University of Michigan.*

licenses were granted in the court's next session and that Erastus Priest himself was indicted "for selling liquor in less quantities than one quart, without license therefor." (He was found not guilty.)

Already by the time of these vital legal proceedings, Ann Arbor had become, in the words of Beakes, "a village of considerable importance," boasting 150 residents, three stores and three more taverns to compete with Rumsey's Washtenaw Coffee House. In December 1829, one of those tavern-keepers, Samuel Camp, advertised in Ann Arbor's first newspaper, the *Western Emigrant*, that he, in partnership with L. Hawley, had built a distillery and promised to "keep constantly on hand, a superior quality of rectified whiskey," which the two would sell by the gallon or barrel or exchange for grain "on liberal terms."

The practice of bartering whiskey for grain and vice versa was common, regardless of one's personal attitudes. One prominent citizen apparently known for "strong temperance principles" also advertised in the *Emigrant* for "a few thousands bushel of grain, for which a fair price will be paid in goods or whiskey." The 1881 history helpfully explains that "in the good old days whisky was regarded as a necessity which no one could do without" and "a legitimate article of commerce."

published in 1924, characterized the time this way:

ttlers of Ann Arbor were, as a rule, the peers of the
..... of any locality on earth but...it was the custom of the
majority of men to indulge in the use, to a greater or lesser degree, of
intoxicating liquors. No barn raising in this or any other locality was
complete without the free dispensing of whisky or other strong drink. In
fact, from many of the influential men of the day, when suggestion was
offered that the offending liquors be omitted and the frames raised by the
strong arms of the men without its invigorating assistance, the almost
universal reply was, "it can't be did."

That was the attitude facing Luther Boyden of Webster, a settlement
north of Ann Arbor, in 1830. Concerned with "the alarming effects of the
free use of whisky," he had helped organize a temperance society in which
he and the other members pledged to "abstain altogether from the use of
whisky as a beverage" (they apparently did not even try to get anyone to give
up beer or cider). This society "did much toward the suppression of the vice
of intemperance."

Trouble was, Boyden needed the help of many men to build a barn on his
property, and as we've seen, it "was an unheard of thing to attempt to raise a
building without whisky." Boyden offered in lieu of liquor a "good supper,"
and with this "innovation on an old established custom," he and the laborers
he recruited successfully "raised the first barn in Webster without whisky."
In his later years, Boyden apparently looked back with satisfaction on this
episode as one of his life's signal achievements.

Not everyone was as successful as Boyden. A few months later, another
gentleman, name of William Lemmon, attempted the same feat in Lima,
near Chelsea. Neighbors came out to help build the Lemmon family home,
but when they were offered water instead of whiskey after completing the
first floor, they laid down their tools and left the hapless man to stew in his
temperance principles. It took the intervention of General Asa Williams,
a local man with pull, to get the rest of the house built. The good general
explained that Lemmon's children did not deserve to go without a roof over
their heads because of their father's "fanaticism."

All this whiskey talk is not to say that there were no beer drinkers among Ann Arbor's earliest residents. In 1829, some of the more civic-minded among them got together to build the town's first municipal building, a jailhouse, constructed on land donated by Rumsey (who had died in 1827) for the purpose. Upon completion, it was necessary for the rather rudimentary wood-frame facility to be inspected before the town's lawmen could start filling it with crooks and ne'er-do-wells.

According to a contemporary account, the crew of jurymen assigned this task proved to be some right jolly fellows, "loving a little fun when there was nothing else to do." They had drafted their own bylaws, imposing fines on one another for various offenses, such as being absent at roll call, to be paid in quantities of beer, which they also demanded from members with no prior jury experience as a sort of initiation fee.

When the time came to inspect the jailhouse, they all marched in file behind their foreman, Colonel Orrin White, and secretary, General Edward Clark. Inside, White and Clark opened the cell door and stepped inside, whereupon the jurymen slammed and locked the door.

"Do you see a gallon of beer each?" they demanded, peering into the cell through the door's spyhole. White and Clark at first ignored the prank, proceeding about the business for which they had come. But the jurymen would not let them out until each man promised that he'd come across with the brew, which they eventually agreed to do.

Turnabout was fair play. Once the door was unlocked and the jokesters sauntered into the cell to begin their inspection, White and Clark slipped out and, in turn, locked them all in, not opening the door until the same ransom of one gallon of beer per man was agreed to, which it again was.

Their clowning done, the jury reported back to the court that the jail was ready for any guests the authorities wanted to send there, and although the same contemporary account notes that "[n]o prisoner ever escaped from it only by 'due process of law,'" historian Orlando Stephenson later wrote in his 1927 tome *Ann Arbor: The First Hundred Years* that "no one could be sure that a prisoner who had been placed within its confines on any particular night would be found there the next morning."

The new jailhouse, commissioned less than seven years later, was built out of brick by a presumably more professional group of beer drinkers.

New Brewery.

A. KERN avails himself of this method of informing his friends and the public generally, that he has commenced the BREW-ING BUSINESS in Ann Arbor, Upper Village, where he intends keeping constantly on hand, for sale, a supply of *STRONG* and *TABLE BEER.* Having had considerable experience in the above business, he flatters himself that he will be able to give entire satisfaction to all those, who may favor him with their patronage.

All orders thankfully received and promptly attended to. **A. KERN.**

Ann Arbor, Feb. 1838. 3w51

The first ad for a commercial brewery in Ann Arbor appeared in the *Michigan Argus* of February 8, 1838. *Ann Arbor District Library.*

"For sale, a supply of strong and table beer," read the advertisement in the February 8, 1838 *Michigan Argus*, in which an A. Kern informed readers that he had "commenced the brewing business in Ann Arbor, Upper Village," or somewhere near today's downtown. Ann Arborites were soon enjoying the first commercial batches of beer to be brewed within the borders of their burgeoning settlement, now a respectable town of four thousand.

Unfortunately, next to nothing is known about Kern's operation or many of Ann Arbor's earliest breweries, which began appearing one by one in the 1830s and 1840s. They had names that, like Kern, were of English, Irish or Scotch origin: Bardwell, Brown, Gordon, Hooper and Ingalls.

These breweries were small in scope, producing on the order of what today a dedicated homebrewer might make. They brewed only ale, owing not just to English tradition but also to the fact that lager brewing did not develop in America until later on, as more and more Germans immigrated to their new homes (more on this in the next chapter). Distribution would have been in buckets, casks or kegs (bottling being too difficult and expensive at the time) and likely not extended much beyond the brewers' immediate neighborhoods.

The ale of the time was not quite like the ales we know and love today. The basic ingredients and brewing techniques were familiar, but the role of yeast was not well understood by brewers, nor was the importance of sanitation. As a result, one was just as likely to get a mugful of sour, contaminated swill as something palatable. The lack of artificial refrigeration and methods of carbonation also guaranteed a product that in any case would be relatively warm and flat. According to beer historian Maureen Ogle, anyone who could afford it would have wanted to opt for imported stout or porter from the more advanced British brewers. It's doubtful that the modern rallying cry of "drink local beer!" would have been too persuasive to the imbibers of this period.

At any rate, none of Ann Arbor's early ale makers lasted long, vanishing into the mists of history after only a year or two and leaving behind no other record of their existence. But one ale brewery that came a little later, Hooper, was so successful that it persisted in various forms for more than a decade.

THE HOOPER BREWERY

Englishman Richard Hooper purchased a parcel of land at the corner of State and Fuller (today's High) Streets in 1856 with the intent of opening a modern brewery in partnership with his son Frederick. By 1858, R. Hooper & Son, "Manufacturer of Ale & Porter and Dealer in Malt & Hops," was in business. The brewery flourished for a time—Hooper was said to have "made a fortune"—on the town's north side until Richard's death in 1866, whereupon the business passed to Frederick and his brother, Charles, who continued brewing under the name Ann Arbor Brewery.

The brothers were still at the helm in 1868, now employing a gentleman by the very German name of Joseph Ambruster. Perhaps the Hoopers were looking to supplement their ale and porter offerings with lager, which by this time was fast becoming the dominant style among beer drinkers.

Whatever the case, the Hooper brothers seem to have thrown in the towel a few years later. Reading the changing demands of consumers, the next owners of the brewery, Thomas F. Hill and Charles A. Chapin, advertised themselves as "Brewers of Ale, Porter and Lager Beer" in the 1872 city directory. Although historian Orlando Stephenson described him as being "for years one of Ann Arbor's leading business men," there is nothing to

21

indicate that Chapin had any background in brewing, and the enterprise folded soon after, likely one of the many victims of the financial panic and ensuing depression of 1873.

The old building stood silent and vacant at the corner of State and Fuller long after brewing ceased. In 1884, the Michigan Central Railroad purchased the land, planning to spend more than $33,000 to demolish the deteriorating brewery and its outbuildings to make room for a bridge and a lavish new depot (what is today the Gandy Dancer restaurant).

Before the demolition team could begin its work, however, a cross-section of Ann Arbor's youth decided to get a head start. An item in the May 27, 1885 *Ann Arbor Courier* wryly noted that the neighborhood boys were "saving the M.C.R.R. folks the trouble of the job" as they picked apart the place, each hoping to triumphantly take home "a trophy from the old brewery."

The building presented problems for the real wrecking crew once it finally got down to business the following spring. "A German workman was badly injured last Thursday, by the premature tumbling in of a wall of the old Hooper brewery that he was assisting in demolishing," noted the April 7, 1886 *Courier*.

Even after the brewery was cleared away and the railroad projects built, a surviving outbuilding was the scene of a sad denouement to the brief Hooper beer dynasty. Reported the *Ann Arbor Argus* of March 20, 1891:

> *A disgraceful cock fight, witnessed by Ann Arbor, Ypsilanti, and Detroit sports, is said to have occurred Tuesday night in the old unused brewery building near the railroad track. The birds were from the three cities and several were killed. No one having any respect for himself was present.*

Although even that scandalous last vestige of the brewery is long gone, the Greek Revival house that the Hooper family lived in still stands on the corner of East Ann and State Streets, once believed to be haunted by the ghost of one of Richard's sons who committed suicide. Maybe the Hooper dynasty continues after all.

Chapter 2

"MOST OF THESE PEOPLE DRANK THEIR LAGER"

E manuel Josenhans sipped his beer and read with interest the letter from his brother-in-law, Johann Heinrich Mann. Mann wrote from across the ocean that he saw incredible opportunity in the Michigan Territory. Land, he said, was plentiful and cheap compared to in Württemberg. He could readily ply his trade as a tanner in the sparsely settled Washtenaw countryside, which fairly teemed with deer, and sell his leathers in the populous area of nearby Detroit city.

In fact, Mann wrote, one could pursue whichever vocation he chose—and even marry the woman he preferred whenever he pleased—and expect no interference from guild, church or political authority. He even detailed the route to follow—over the Atlantic to New York, through the Erie Canal into the vast lake of the same name and thus over to Detroit—should others choose to emigrate after him, which he wholeheartedly recommended.

Josenhans did not think that he would make the trip to the New World himself, but the letter's contents nevertheless sounded encouraging to him. He shared them with the rest of the family and all his friends in Stuttgart. Whether they were farmers, bakers, brewers, shoemakers or mechanics, he believed that they would find what Mann had to say as intriguing as he had. Perhaps, he thought, some of them would even wish to follow Mann's advice and seek new lives in this Michigan for themselves.

German immigration to Washtenaw County began around 1830 and continued in earnest for the next one hundred years. Many of the early families undertaking the long, difficult and often perilous journey across the sea came from Swabia, a distinct region in the southwest of the country whose largest and most well-known city is Stuttgart. Today, the region, which encompasses a large portion of the state of Baden-Württemberg, is prosperous, but beginning in the early and mid-nineteenth century and lasting for decades, there was much political repression, social unrest and economic uncertainty.

Family ties and word of mouth were major factors drawing many of the Swabian immigrants to the Washtenaw region in particular. A large number of them settled in Ann Arbor, predominantly in the old Second Ward or what is known today as the Old West Side, but many others went farther west to start farms and other businesses in places like Manchester and Dexter, as well as Lima, Lodi and Freedom Townships.

According to Ann Arbor historian Grace Shackman, in 1832 there were more than thirty Swabian families in the area. Pastor Friedrich Schmid, who came over in 1833 to minister to the growing Lutheran flock and later founded many Michigan churches, described Ann Arbor in a letter to his European superiors as "a little village, mainly of English people, only a few German families are in the city, the remaining families, perhaps forty to forty-six, live out in the woods and forest."

By 1855, more than 5,000 mostly Swabian Germans called Washtenaw County home (Ann Arbor proper had an overall population of only about 4,800 at that time), and from that point on, the large, well-established German-speaking population began to draw more and more immigrants from regions outside Swabia. The Franco-Prussian War of 1870–71, followed by Otto von Bismarck's political centralization and domination of the formerly independent German states, only accelerated the influx.

Historian Orlando Stephenson noted in *Ann Arbor: The First Hundred Years* that the earliest arriving Germans tended to keep to themselves and initially had little influence on the affairs of the town. But as time went on and the immigrants' children grew and became more assimilated, things quickly changed.

"Most of these people drank their lager beer," wrote Stephenson, continuing with great cultural sensitivity, "but, unlike some of the Irish, their business failures were few and they were never fond of either the stronger alcoholic beverages or the litigations which too frequently followed when the sons of Erin imbibed too freely."

The result of this German moderation and industriousness was that the native-born villagers came to accept and even respect the newcomers for the most part, although continuously escalating religious, cultural and political tensions would lead to tumultuous conflicts in the ensuing decades, as will be seen.

The German influence on Ann Arbor's development over the years was ultimately profound. Families—including those with still-familiar names like Schlenker, Allmendinger, Metzger, Muehlig, Hutzel, Schlanderer and Vogel—founded churches, tended farms, started businesses, formed social organizations and introduced their distinct customs to their adopted homeland.

Of course, the most important of these customs as regards our present narrative was the German reverence for beer. And "reverence" is not too strong a word. Beer historian Maureen Ogle noted how beer was "central to German culture," tracing as far back as Old Norse sagas that memorialized fermented beverages as a gift from the gods. Beer for the German immigrants was not just a recreational drink; it was entwined with practically every imaginable social function, reinforcing wedding vows, ending disagreements and closing contracts.

The German newcomers also brought with them something that would completely change the character of beer in America and, indeed, the world: the knowledge of how to make a newer, tastier variety of it that had begun in Bavaria and was already gaining in popularity on the European continent.

———•——

It is a matter of some debate as to just when and where the first batch of lager beer was brewed in America, but there is no doubt that the new style was introduced to these shores by immigrant brewers in the early 1840s and spread rapidly thereafter. The time was ripe for this crisp, clean brew to sweep a new continent, too, thanks to a confluence of factors.

Foremost among these factors was the development of the fast-sailing clipper ship, which cut the time of sea voyages from Europe to America from months to weeks. This was crucial, according to beer historian Gregg Smith, because lager yeast, even when stored under ideal conditions,

The saloon of George W. Cady (third from left) at what is now part of Sidetrack Bar & Grill in Ypsilanti's Depot Town. *Sam Sturgis Collection, Bentley Historical Library, University of Michigan.*

remained viable for only about thirty days. Before the clipper era, none of those beautiful little beer beasties could even make it over to the New World alive to do their important work.

Other factors favorable to the spread of lager beer included continuing technical advances in refrigeration (vital for cold-fermenting lager yeast), transportation and brewing methods in general. It also helped that the clear, sparkling beer produced by lager yeast appealed much more to the senses than the muddy and oft-spoiled ales that many drinkers spurned in favor of cider and spirits.

Plus, according to Smith, the light-bodied, easy-drinking brew was a perfect fit with good old-fashioned American gluttony: a person could down many more of them in a sitting than was customary with the heavier ales—or, of course, with strong spirits. (Lager's light, low-alcohol profile would eventually lead anti-prohibitionists to argue for beer as the true drink of temperance and moderation.)

Add the aforementioned massive wave of thirsty German immigrants and the great American lager revolution was on.

THREE EARLY LAGER BREWERS

One of the first German names to appear in Ann Arbor brewing history is that of Frederick Ruoff, who is listed in the city directory of 1860 (the first to be issued) as proprietor of the Bavarian Brewery, which he ran from his home located on Fuller between State and Elizabeth Streets, putting him within a block or two of the Hooper brewery. It seems plausible—given his surname, the era in which he founded his brewery and the specific region he named it after (Bavaria being the epicenter of lager brewing)—that Ruoff could have brewed Ann Arbor's first lagers.

The Bavarian Brewery lasted until about 1872 (when it was then listed simply as Ruoff's brewery), but it seems never to have grown beyond a home-based concern. By the time of the next city directory, Ruoff and his brewery are gone. Different accounts conclude that he was driven out of business in the 1873 panic that ended the brewing careers of Messieurs Hill and Chapin and many others, although curiously, he is still listed in the 1875 *Michigan Gazetteer and Business Directory*. Peter Blum noted in *Brewed in Detroit* that Frederick Ruoff was likely related to August Ruoff, who arrived in Detroit from Swabia in 1849 and started the Ruoff Brewing Company there in 1861.

Another, perhaps stronger, candidate for Ann Arbor's first lager brewer is Gottlieb (G.F.) Hauser, who advertised "Beer and Lager Beer" for sale from his brewery on "First Street, Near Liberty" in the 1860 city directory.

A panoramic map of Ann Arbor in 1880. *Ann Arbor District Library.*

BEECK&HELL, LITH. MILWAUKEE, WIS.

CITY OF

RBOR,

N. 1880

610,658

UNIVERSITIES OF MICHIGAN.

23. University Hall.
24. Department of Law.
25. Department of Medicine and Surgery
26. Hospital—Alopathic.
27. Homœopathic Medical College and Hospital.
28. Chemical Laboratory.
29. Dental College.
30. Museum of Science.
31. Museum of Art and History.
32. BotlieHouse.
33. Astronomical Observatory.
34. Presidents House.
35. Steam Carpenter's Shop,

36. Carriage & Sleigh Factory, C. Walker & Bros., Prop.
37. Carriage & Sleigh Fact'y, B. F. Arksey, Prop
38.   "   "   A. R. Schmidt, "
39. Sash, Door & Blind Fact'y, Luick Bros.,Prop
40.   "   "   "   H. Krapf, Prop.
41. Cabinet Fact'y, Rauschenberger & Co., Prop.
42. Triumph Wind Mill Factory, A. M. Bodwell, Prop.
43. Soap and Potash Factory, J. Birk, Prop.
44. Tannery, J. Heinzman & Son, Prop.
45.   "   Henry Krause, Prop.
46. Ferdon Lumber Yard, Jas. Tolbert, Prop.
47. Marble Yard, Anton Eisell, Prop.
48. Cook House, C. H. & F. W. Jewell, Prop.
49. Hotel.
50. Agricultural Ware House, M. Rogers, Prop.
51. Green House, Cousins & Hall, Prop.
52.   "   Jas. Toms, Prop.

G411
.A8I
188
.R8
Rug

Either Hauser or a previous owner recognized early on the advantages of locating near both a major thoroughfare (Liberty Street) and a good source of water (Allen's Creek). According to architectural historians Marjorie Reade and Susan Wineberg, an 1853 map of Ann Arbor already showed the designation "brewery" at this site.

Hauser and his partner and brother, Christian, sited their brewery on a sloping lot such that Peter Brehm and other workers could enter the basement lagering caves from a ground-level ingress. They also made use of the cool water from the creek to help keep the conditioning beers at a low enough temperature to allow the lager yeast to work its magic.

Christian Hauser sold his interest in the brewery and left for Philadelphia not long after. Ownership of the brewery then passed to John Reyer by 1868, when it was listed as the City Brewery, and it changed hands again in about 1872 to August and Fridotus Ekhardt, who renamed it Ekhardt Brothers. According to Reade and Wineberg, the Ekhardts, too, went out of business the following year in the Panic of 1873. The Ann Arbor Central Mills took over the building in 1882, but a beer distributorship seems to have been part of the property in that decade; Reade and Wineberg cite an 1886 ad promising to deliver Schlitz and Detroit Peninsular Brewery Company beer "to any part of the city, daytime or evening."

The original brewery building is gone (as is Allen's Creek, which was enclosed in a storm drain in 1926), but Ann Arborites know the arched brick lager caves today as the Cavern Club, the basement bar of the building complex that also houses the Circus and Millennium nightclubs.

Besides Ruoff and Hauser, Lawrence Trube is the other brewer listed in the 1860 city directory, residing on Fifth Avenue; nothing further is seen of him beyond this single entry. (The name Lawrence "Traub" appears sometime later in connection with an unnamed brewery in Manchester, but one can only speculate if it's the same person.)

Because of his address on Fifth, Reade and Wineberg place Trube at the Central Brewery that operated at the intersection of Fifth and Summit. This may be the case, although sources conflict as to when brewing commenced at this location. Reade and Wineberg date the original brewery building to 1858 (with an 1898 renovation); Blum to 1865.

The building's gabled roof is unusual for a brewery of that time, and Ann Arbor historian Wystan Stevens told of tunnels underneath that at one point were used as runoff for water from a nearby spring. Blum estimated that the structure had a maximum capacity of about five thousand barrels, but how much it actually produced is not known.

Whatever became of Trube, by 1868 John Volz is unambiguously listed as the Central Brewery's proprietor in the city directory. He seems not to have done particularly well in the business, and a 1968 *Huron Valley Ad-Visor* feature by Margaret Murawski notes that Volz took out several mortgages on his land in order to finance the construction of a stately Italianate mansion next to the brewery. Unfortunately, his timing was terrible, and the combination of debt and the economic crisis in 1873 ruined him. To pay the bills, Volz sold first the brewery to Jacob Beck and then, a few years later, the house.

Beck and his partners embarked on a vigorous campaign to revive the flagging brewery. They renovated the brewhouse, replaced all the equipment and hired and advertised (in the 1875 *Michigan State Gazetteer*) "a Cincinnati brewer with many years [*sic*] experience" who would enable them to "furnish lager beer second to none." Cincinnati at the time rivaled St. Louis and Milwaukee as a well-known lager-producing powerhouse, so the new owners clearly meant business.

But their business lasted only another few years, and by 1883, the building housed a soft drink bottler. In the twentieth century, it was converted into a tenement that by the 1920s was so full of Italian immigrants that locals took to calling it "Little Italy." Today, the ivy-covered edifice is a more upscale apartment building going by the name of the Old Brewery, still standing next to the Italianate mansion of its onetime owner John Volz.

CHAPTER 3

THE BEER BARONETS OF ANN ARBOR

bar ·on ·et: noun. the holder of a rank of honor below a baron and above a knight.

Peter Brehm was ready to start his own business. After only a few short years in Ann Arbor, he had a beautiful wife and a job at the City Brewery making lager beer, which, now that it was catching on even among the non-German townsfolk, offered what he knew to be a sizeable opportunity. He had been talking with John Reyer about starting a new brewery, one that would be bigger than City and produce a better lager, something closer to what he remembered drinking back in his native Bavaria.

He and Reyer already knew the most desirable spot on which to build, too: several blocks to the south and west of Hauser's brewery, not too close but close enough to make good use of the same creek water that cooled the *bierkeller* at City.

Life in Ann Arbor had already been good to him, but he was thirty-five years old, and if he was ever really going to make his mark, then the time was now.

———

"Beer baron" is the term often applied to the owners of America's largest and most successful breweries of the nineteenth century. It seems a fitting

Beer delivery to Charles Binder's saloon at 112 West Liberty Street, circa 1880. *Sam Sturgis Collection, Bentley Historical Library, University of Michigan.*

description for titans like Adolphus Busch, whose rapidly expanding Anheuser-Busch brewery sold more than 131,000 barrels of beer in 1880 on its way to becoming the largest brewery in the world. By contrast, Ann Arbor's biggest and most successful breweries of the time, the Western Brewery and the Northern Brewery, produced only about 5,400 barrels that same year combined.

Yet it makes sense to distinguish the relative success of the people who ran these two long-lasting brewing operations from the city's earlier, smaller brewers of yore. They lasted for decades and filled a niche in between the days of the home-based or small-scale neighborhood breweries and the later dominance of the big regional and national beer brands. Call them the beer baronets.

The Western Brewery

Tree Town's first beer baronet was, without a doubt, Peter Brehm, "a pioneer in the brewery business of Ann Arbor," in the words of the 1881 county history. Born in Bavaria in 1825, Brehm immigrated to Ann Arbor by way of Canada in 1856. With his tall stature, dark hair, Van Dyke beard and penetrating eyes, he soon attracted the attention of a young widow, Louisa Muehlig, and they were married the following year. He worked for a time at the City Brewery and then in 1861 founded the Western Brewery in partnership with John Reyer. It stood on Fourth Street between Liberty and West Madison, near where the Bach Elementary School is now, and produced lager beer.

The business partners were just getting into their groove when disaster struck and a fire burned the whole brewery to the ground in 1864. But like any good entrepreneur, Brehm was undeterred and set about replacing the destroyed brewery with an even larger one, two stories in height with a cellar and measuring about sixty by thirty feet. Even though the business thrived, in a few years, Reyer wanted out. He sold his interest to Brehm to buy the City Brewery on First Street from Gottlieb Hauser.

By 1870, Brehm was doing so well that he could afford to build a beautiful mansion on West Liberty Street, just around the corner from his former partner's brewery. The new solid red brick house, with its handsomely curved mansard roof, had all the hallmarks of affluence and provided space and comfort for the Brehm family, which in addition to Louisa's daughter from her first marriage, Caroline, now included a young son, Gustave.

Perhaps it was his newfound domestic bliss or the fact that he was by now well into his forties, but Brehm seemingly lost interest in running the brewery in the early 1870s. He next rented the operation out to brewer Fred Kirn, who took over for a brief period.

On the afternoon of February 28, 1873, a gunshot echoed up and down West Liberty Street. The cold winter air was rent with the subsequent cries of Louisa Brehm, sounding from the mansard roofed house. Peter's bloody corpse lay in their bedroom, dead with a bullet hole through his head, the pistol he used smoking on the floor by his hand.

The circumstances leading up to Peter Brehm's suicide are mysterious and hint at something darker in his life. The March 7 edition of the *Michigan Argus* reported that he "had for some time been laboring under a sort of mania induced by hard drinking." The *Peninsular Courier and Family Visitant* gave a more detailed but no less puzzling account:

The mansard-roofed home of Western Brewery founder Peter Brehm as it looked in the 1870s. *Sam Sturgis Collection, Bentley Historical Library, University of Michigan.*

The particulars of the melancholy death of Peter Brehm, late proprietor of the Western Brewery, are these: Mr. Brehm, when suffering from temporary insanity, thought that he should be sued by some one, he knew not who. Last Friday he came home and informed his wife that he had been sued and must go to court. Changing his clothes, he started towards the Court House, but soon returned, and going directly to his room, shot himself through his head, dying instantly. Mr. Brehm was a kind-hearted and very generous man, respected by all who knew him.

Following the "very largely attended" funeral, Peter Brehm was laid to rest at Forest Hill Cemetery on Observatory Road.

Frank Ruck next rented the Western Brewery from the widow Brehm and brewed, according to an 1877 ad, "none but the very best quality of lager beer." The 1881 county history recorded that Ruck was born in Germany in 1843 and there "learned the business of brewing" before immigrating in 1861 to Cincinnati, where he brewed for the next eight years. He came to Ann Arbor

The Western Brewery supplied beer to many downtown businesses, such as Lewis Kurtz's saloon at 120 West Liberty Street. *Sam Sturgis Collection, Bentley Historical Library, University of Michigan.*

in 1874, and although the records make no mention of it, he was probably the "Cincinnati brewer" hired at Jacob Beck's ill-fated Central Brewery.

In 1880, Ruck left to take over the Southern Brewery in Manchester, and Louisa Brehm sold her husband's former business to "two enterprising young Germans of Ann Arbor," Christian Martin and Matthias Fischer. Like Ruck before him, Martin trained as a brewer in his native Germany, where he was born in 1854. He immigrated in 1871 to Battle Creek and then migrated to Ann Arbor in 1875. None of the county histories provides any details on Matthias Fischer.

The new owners immediately began "building up quite an extensive trade," using in their first year 1,500 bushels of malt, 1,700 pounds of hops, 225 cords of wood and eight hundred tons of ice in producing three thousand barrels of beer that found "a ready sale in all parts of the county."

Martin and Fischer gradually expanded and updated the brewery. The June 3, 1885 *Ann Arbor Courier* reported that the owners were "re-laying the pipes that supply that institution with water from the spring on the hill to the Southwest of the city." In 1891, they upgraded the brewhouse by putting in a "very large" new copper kettle and boiler. By 1899, the brewery had two icehouses that held 1,800 tons of ice, giving some indication of how much more beer it was producing.

In 1902, the business was reorganized as the Michigan Union Brewing Company, named for the bartenders and brewers union representing the employees, with Lewis Kurtz, who also owned a saloon on West Liberty Street, as president and Christian Martin as treasurer. A new four-story brick building was erected slightly to the north of the original location to further ramp up annual production, which by 1906 had reached thirty-five thousand barrels. A bottling operation was also added, with the brewery offering its beer in cases of what would be called, in the parlance of our times, "bombers."

Like other breweries of the era, the Michigan Union's brewhouse was designed to occupy the top part of the building. According to a lengthy 1975 *Ann Arbor News* feature by Mary Hunt, a wood- or coal-fired boiler generated the steam used to both power the ice machine and heat the ten-foot-wide copper brew kettle. When the boil was complete, the filtered wort was transferred via gravity to the "upper cellar" on the next floor down. There it was cooled before the yeast was pitched, and it was transferred to the next cellar to ferment in three-thousand-gallon barrels. The carbon dioxide generated during fermentation was siphoned into another, cave-like lagering cellar and forced into previous batches of beer stored there for carbonation. The whole process from brew to bottle took about five weeks.

Martin continued his role as brewmaster, while Fischer was in charge of the packaging operations, including bottling. Martin and his brewers, Mike Wiedmann and son Caspar Wiedmann, got their day started at 4:00 or 5:00 a.m. because it took twelve hours just to move a batch of wort from the mash tun to the fermenter. Fortunately, Martin's commute was short—according to Ann Arbor historian Grace Shackman, he lived in a house right across the street.

The business was run informally, with everyone pitching in and helping in any needed capacity and the children of employees coming in to work alongside their fathers. Shackman recounted how the son of one of the architects who built the new brewery remembered being sent to fetch beer in buckets to serve to the construction crew. Matthias Fischer's son, Bill, recalled in Hunt's article how he used to get a glass of beer when he dropped his father's lunch off at the brewery in the morning on his way to school.

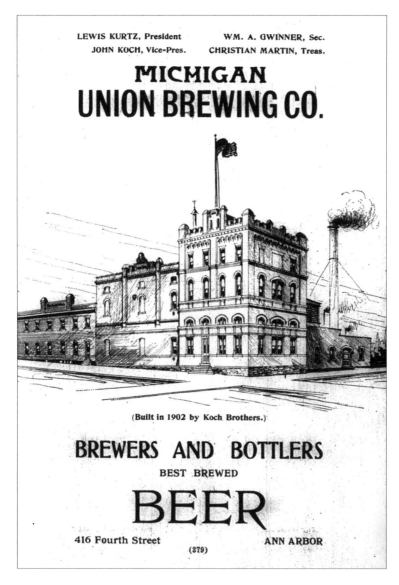

A somewhat fanciful drawing of the new Michigan Union brewery from the 1903 Ann Arbor City Directory. *Ann Arbor District Library.*

Michigan Union Brewing continued to grow, expanding its distribution from just Dexter and Saline to include (thanks to newfangled automobiles) Milan and Whitmore Lake, until the state adopted full prohibition in 1918 and put an end to Ann Arbor's beer baronet era.

THE NORTHERN BREWERY

The other brewery in town during this period was the Northern Brewery, founded in 1872 by George Krause. It stood on Mill Street, now Jones Drive, in "Lower Town" off of Plymouth Road, north of the Huron River on the Broadway hill. Krause did not stick around long. According to the 1881 county history, he sold the business to the Frey brothers, John and Fred, within a year. Former City Brewery partner Christian Hauser, recently returned to Ann Arbor after losing his money in a bank collapse, joined the enterprise as bookkeeper.

The young brothers annually took in five thousand bushels of grain and four thousand pounds of hops to produce about 2,400 barrels of their beer. Brewery workers dammed nearby Traver Creek to form a pond behind the building, from which they harvested ice in the winter to stock the icehouse and refrigerate the lagering brew throughout the warm months.

Fred sold out his interest in the brewery to John in 1873, and at some point thereafter, another Frey brother, Christian, came on board. The business boomed for the next decade, but tragedy lurked just around the corner. The September 10, 1884 *Ann Arbor Courier* sadly reported the untimely passing of John Frey, age thirty-seven, of "quick consumption." Christian, age forty-one, followed his brother into the hereafter a few months later due to the same malady. (Bookkeeper Hauser lived to the ripe age of seventy but died in 1898 after a lengthy stay in a Pontiac asylum, a victim of "cancer of the jaw.") Christian Frey's obituary notice concluded that he and John "were good business men in their line."

"An Ypsilantian has bought the northern brewery of the Frey estate for $11,000," announced the *Ann Arbor Courier* of April 22, 1885. That Ypsilantian was Herman Hardinghaus, who before becoming an Ypsilantian was a Prussian (born there in 1846) and Cincinnatian, where he initially settled in 1864. A brewer's son who had apprenticed to the trade in Germany, he served as a partner in the L.Z. Foerster brewery on Ypsilanti's Grove Street for about nine years before moving to Ann Arbor to take over the Northern.

Hardinghaus set about making improvements, replacing the frame buildings of the Freys' era with a two-story brick structure that, with alterations and additions, remains today. It was, according to county historian Samuel Beakes, "a fine plant, having a large capacity" from which the brewers "manufacture a fine bottle beer, enjoying an extensive trade."

To bolster that trade, Hardinghaus initiated an aggressive marketing campaign, touting his "celebrated export beer" with attractive newspaper ads. This beer was an ale, "bottled expressly for table use" and shipped to

Workers at the Northern Brewery, then known as the Ann Arbor Brewing Company, in the 1890s. The little girl is Ernest Rehberg's daughter. *Doug Smith.*

other cities and towns. Historian Wystan Stevens in a lengthy 1973 feature on the brewery, from which much of this account is drawn, explained why the bottling works were located in a separate building across the street: it was due to the wacky way beer was taxed at the time. For whatever reason, the feds required barrels (taxed one dollar apiece) to be filled in the brewery and then specifically transported across a public road before being put into bottles.

Hardinghaus relied on his talented and energetic brewmaster, Ernest Rehberg, who had been with the company since 1884. Rehberg was born in Detroit in 1859 to Prussian parents. He worked in Jacob Mann's brewery, and "there learned the trade, which he thoroughly mastered in principle and detail," according to Beakes. In 1884, he came to Ann Arbor, where he became active in local affairs, "taking a helpful interest in progressive measures." He was, in fact, so interested in progressive measures that he ran for and was elected to a two-year term on the city council in 1892.

That same year, the Northern Brewery was reorganized into a stock company capitalized with $40,000. Proving that beer was in the blood, Peter

Brehm's now-grown son, Gustave, joined Hardinghaus, Rehberg and two others as stockholders in the new company, which was renamed Ann Arbor Brewing Company. Rehberg took the reins as president, while Hardinghaus assumed a vice-president role and Brehm became secretary and treasurer. The new management team had an ambitious goal, announced in the January 6, 1893 *Ann Arbor Argus*: "to manufacture a quality of beer that will successfully compete with any domestic or imported beer on the market."

In 1897, there was another reorganization. Gustave Brehm, who had taken on a role as proprietor of a saloon affiliated with the brewery, skipped town completely after leaving behind a note for his wife and children advising them that he was not coming back. Ann Arbor Brewing's stockholders elected Rehberg president and treasurer and Hardinghaus vice-president and secretary.

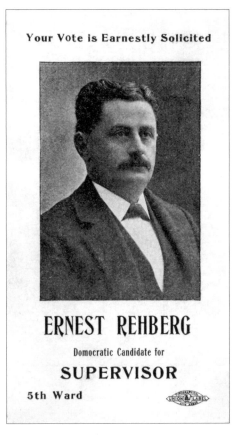

Your Vote is Earnestly Solicited

ERNEST REHBERG

Domocratic Candidate for

SUPERVISOR

5th Ward

UNION LABEL

The Northern Brewery's Ernest Rehberg mixed beer with politics, winning a seat on the Ann Arbor City Council in 1892. *Doug Smith.*

They, along with Ernest's brother, Louis, also served as directors. According to Beakes, the indefatigable Rehberg's role was actually even more extensive; he was "practical manager of the enterprise," where "his thorough understanding of the business in every department enables him to carry it forward along…successful lines."

Rehberg, Hardinghaus and company again aggressively marketed their products, exhorting readers of the *Argus* to "buy pure beer!" and to try "a good warm weather drink" and "the best beer you can drink." They boasted of their export and lager beer: "Give it a trial and you will use no other."

The strategy initially paid off. Despite stiff local competition from Martin and Fischer's Western Brewery—as well as increasing encroachment

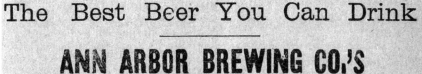

The Best Beer You Can Drink

ANN ARBOR BREWING CO.'S
Pure Export and Lager Beer

Send in your orderfor
a case or keg.

Give it a trial and you
will use no other.

Both Phones No. 101

Advertisement in an 1899 issue of the *Ann Arbor Argus-Democrat. Ann Arbor District Library.*

from big regional breweries like Stroh, Schlitz and Pabst—the Ann Arbor Brewing Company beers found their place in the market. The company was successful enough that by 1894 Hardinghaus was able to build a new house for $5,000 on Kingsley Street.

But success would prove to be fleeting. Within a decade, Rehberg left to run a saloon, Hardinghaus died and Machiavellian power struggles among the stockholders plagued a company that was being quickly overcome by the growing clout of the regionals. Rehberg came back in 1904 and reorganized the business as a partnership with former bookkeeper Lewis Roberts. They renamed it Ann Arbor City Brewery, but the writing was on the wall. Far from offering the best beer one could drink, the company's ads now merely looked to "solicit your patronage" and "endeavor to please you," and the brewery closed up shop for good in 1908.

Rehberg and his son, Carl, turned to a business that had been a sideline during the brewing years and made it their full-time occupation: ice. They

The former Northern Brewery at 1327 Jones Drive as it looks today. *Photo by David Bardallis.*

founded the Artificial Ice Company, the first company in Ann Arbor to manufacture ice rather than harvest it; it operated until 1964, well into the time that home refrigerators meant that the iceman no longer needed to cometh. In a bit of irony, the company went back to its beer roots toward the end, becoming a distributor of Schlitz and Old Milwaukee from 1955 on.

In 1926, Carl Rehberg also started the Arbor Springs Water Company, which bottled and delivered water from the spring that once fed the brewery. That business continues today, situated on Jones Drive next to Hardinghaus's old brick building.

As for that building, after the brewery closed, it became home to various companies, including in 1922 the Ann Arbor Foundry Company, which lasted for fifty years. In the 1970s, two architects, Dick Fry and David Peters, renovated the building for office space and, in 1995, sold the property to Doug Smith, who owns it today. Known as the Tech Brewery, it serves as a collaborative workspace for several startup companies.

Smith says that when Fry and Peters bought the building, they were not initially aware that it had a basement. The basement was discovered only during the renovation process, when a crew cut into the floor to install a water line and the dirt collapsed downward into an enormous cavern. Climbing down on a ladder, they discovered a sixty-foot-long tunnel covered

Brewery memorabilia on display in the lobby of 1327 Jones Drive. *Photo by David Bardallis.*

in slag and other industrial residue that ended in a brick archway—the former brewery's old beer caves.

It took years to hand-excavate the basement, during which time a second tunnel was uncovered, and renovation was not completed until after Smith bought the building. Today, the cavernous cellar provides attractive and functional office space in an area once stacked floor to ceiling with barrels of beer. (The current tenants now keep all their beer in a refrigerator in a break area upstairs.)

Smith has over the years collected a number of bottles from Ann Arbor's beer baronet era, including several from the Ann Arbor Brewing Company of Rehberg and Hardinghaus. The bottles are embossed with an advisory that amuses today, arising from a Michigan law of the time that ordered, "Persons engaged in manufacturing, rectifying or preparing [alcoholic beverages] in any way must brand on each barrel, cask, or vessel…the words 'Pure and without drugs or poison.'"

Smith plans to eventually create a full-fledged historical display of bottles, photographs and other memorabilia in the building's lobby, a tribute to one of Ann Arbor's most successful bygone breweries.

CHAPTER 4
BEER IN OLD YPSILANTI

It seemed to Benjamin Woodruff that all the county was there—more than two score of people, old and young, come to celebrate Independence Day on his land.

But that was not the only thing to celebrate. It had been a year almost to the day since he had moved his wife, six children and a servant up from Ohio and into their newly constructed dwelling in the Michigan Territory. The money from his wife's modest inheritance went much further here; they had been able to buy an entire sixty acres by the Huron River and begin a new life.

Neither the stifling, humid summertime air nor the incessantly swarming insects could disturb his festive mood as he surveyed the families gathered here under the sun—the Grants, the Tuttles, the Crosses and many others—all enjoying the provisions he had fetched from Detroit for the occasion. Cheeses, raisins, rice and, of course, a half-barrel of whiskey made for a good start. Now a fire had been sparked for roasting the slaughtered beef, the mud-plastered stone oven was being prepared for baking and he was about ready to take his place atop the large stump and read from the Declaration of Independence to the delight of this merry company.

Yes, life in the tangled territorial wilderness was a constant struggle. But on this day, he could take a moment to enjoy what had been accomplished and imagine how much more would be in the future. Soon, Woodruff's Grove would become the most prosperous and well-known village in the county. He had staked his name on it.

But now for some of that whiskey…

The history of Ann Arbor has been entwined with that of its neighbor ten miles to the southeast, Ypsilanti, ever since the two towns' founding within a year of each other. In fact, Ypsilanti owes its unusual appellation to the man credited with first establishing the University of Michigan, Judge Augustus Woodward, who was impressed by the exploits of General Demetrius Ypsilanti in the Greek War for Independence then raging.

It might not have been so. But for the U.S. surveyors' decision in 1825 to locate the planned Detroit–Chicago road (now Michigan Avenue) through Woodward's plot of land, the earlier settlement of Woodruff's Grove a mile south might have given its name to the present-day city. Instead, that earlier settlement gave its name only to an Ypsilanti street and, nearly half a century later, a brewery on that street.

The Foerster Brewery

The brewery that carried the Foerster name for four decades originally was known as the Grove Brewery and Bottling Company. Two gentlemen with the rather Seussian-sounding monikers of Taufkirth and Trockenbrod built it, the 1881 county history noted, "at a cost of several thousand dollars" sometime in the 1860s. The beer business did not seem to suit Messieurs Taufkirth and Trockenbrod, however, and they sold out of it in 1870 to Louis Ziegler Foerster and his brother Adam.

Louis and Adam came from a large family. They were just two of the ten children born to Ludwig and Margaret Foerster in Ontario, Canada, where they settled after emigrating from Baden, Germany, in 1835. Louis originally worked as a carpenter but gave it up when he arrived in Ypsilanti the same year he and Adam bought the brewery.

At the time of the sale, the brewery near the intersection of South Grove and South Prospect Streets was tiny, selling only about fifty barrels of beer annually. Louis and Adam slowly ramped up production over the next few years until, according to Peter Blum's *Brewed in Detroit*, Adam left the business and moved to Lansing in 1874. In that same year, a local history published in the *Ypsilanti Commercial* noted the brewery's "large cellars which are well stocked with beer which is manufactured here from the best of material and after the most approved manner."

Louis managed by himself for the next two years but then decided that he needed to bring on a new partner. He chose none other than Herman Hardinghaus, the future proprietor of Ann Arbor's Northern Brewery, and that was when the fireworks really started. With German-trained brewer Hardinghaus on board, annual sales climbed to more than two thousand barrels within a few years, and by 1881, that figure had doubled to between four thousand and five thousand barrels.

Ypsilantians loved them some Foerster beer. According to Blum, demand continued to increase, and the brewery, soon known as L.Z. Foerster and Company, needed a larger and more up-to-date facility. The original wood-frame structure was knocked down in 1887 and replaced with a new three-story brick building that was, according to the Beakes county history, "splendidly equipped with the most modern appliances for making beer." The bottling works were located across the street to meet the ridiculous federal standards; from there, workers packaged Gold Band Export, pilsener and porter for shipping "to all parts of Michigan," with the pilsener "known in many other states as well." Blum added that Foerster also brewed a Bavarian lager as well as a bock.

The former Foerster brewery at 414 South Grove Street in Ypsilanti as it looked in 1916, when it was called Hoch Brewing Company. *Ypsilanti Historical Society.*

In 1890, Louis incorporated the business, with himself as president and treasurer and two of his sons, Louis K. and Jacob, vice-president and secretary, respectively. A third son, Albert, also joined the company. Ever driven and looking for ways to improve, the fifty-six-year-old Louis took a leave of absence in 1892 to attend the American Brewing Academy in Chicago (today's Siebel Institute). He had a full course load, studying chemistry, physics, math, "mechanical appliances," bacteriology and biology. When he was through, he received his diploma as master in the art of brewing.

The Foerster brewery continued to hold its own, even after the regional and national beer brands began achieving market domination. The family maintained control until 1914, when, for reasons not clear, Henry Hoch took over, renaming the business Hoch Brewing Company. He struggled to keep it going and was done by 1916, after which time the brewery stood idle through the dark days of prohibition.

Louis Foerster lived to see both the end of his brewery and the beginning of prohibition. He died in 1921 at the age of eighty-five.

SWAINE'S MALT HOUSE

In addition to a successful brewery, nineteenth-century Ypsilanti boasted a thriving malt business. It also began in about 1870, when partners and brothers-in-law Leonard C. Wallington and Worger George converted an old schoolhouse on the corner of North Forest Street and East Forest Avenue into a small malt-house. They were joined a little over a year later by an ambitious young Englishman who married into the family and would take the business to the proverbial next level.

Frederick J. Swaine was born in 1850 in the town of Westerham in Kent County, England. Nothing much is known of his life there, but he must have been a young man of at least some means, as he was able, at the age of twenty-one, to cross the pond to America for a "pleasure trip," which included a stop in Ypsilanti to visit friends. He fell in love with the area and, following a brief return to England, made arrangements to move here.

Things then happened fast. Swaine in short order married Worger's sister, Eliza, and entered into the malting business with his fellow brothers-in-law. In 1872, he bought out Wallington and sometime thereafter George, too, becoming sole owner of the fledgling business. By then, the businessmen

Frederick Swaine's malt house at 111 East Forest Avenue in Ypsilanti supplied ingredients to many local breweries. Swaine died in 1897, and the building was demolished in 1912. *Ypsilanti Historical Society.*

had "already acquired a reputation that brings them orders far beyond their ability to fill," according to the 1874 *Ypsilanti Commercial* history.

To help meet the overwhelming demand, Swaine next expanded his operation by enlarging the converted schoolhouse into a modern, three-story brick malt-house with the equipment to match. The upgrades enabled him to increase production capacity from eleven thousand bushels of barley in 1874 to forty thousand bushels by 1880.

Swaine's malt was used to make beer throughout Ypsilanti, Ann Arbor, Manchester and other points in between. He also dealt in hops, although there are no specific records detailing that side of his business.

Things continued swimmingly for the next seventeen years until Swaine died suddenly in 1897, leaving behind a wife and two daughters. His obituary notice in the April 16 *Ann Arbor Argus* described him as "a prominent citizen" who was active in local politics and whose malt business was well known throughout "this section of the state."

The beautiful Italianate house that the Swaines once occupied on East Forest Avenue still stands, not far from Ypsilanti's modern-day Corner Brewery, but the malt-house next to it was demolished in 1912 following years of decline.

YPSILANTI'S OTHER BREWERIES

Two other breweries operated before the Foersters ever got their start in the business, but little is known of either of them.

Jacob Grob, a German immigrant born in Württemberg in 1839, is recognized as starting the first brewery in Ypsilanti, in 1861. He initially settled with his parents in Monroe, where, according to researcher Kevin Nash, he brewed for a time before moving north. The same year he arrived in Ypsilanti, he built a small brewery by his home on West Forest Avenue and married Sophie Post, with whom he had two daughters. Three years later, he enlarged an existing building into "an extensive ice-house, and supplied many tons of that cooling luxury to the inhabitants of Ypsilanti during the hot and sultry summer months," noted the 1881 county history.

According to Blum, Grob produced 190 barrels of beer in 1878 and may have brewed just once a week on a 4- or 5-barrel system, doing a "good local business" in the words of the *Ypsilanti Commercial*. "The brewings are generally successful," noted the 1881 county history, "and the beer is said to be much appreciated by those who use it."

As the Foerster brewery grew in size and reach, Grob seems to have shifted more and more of his attention to the ice business. In the winter of 1880–81, he was said to have harvested "over 600 cords of ice." It is not known exactly how long the brewery remained in business; Blum has it lasting until 1915.

Even less is known about Ypsilanti's only other brewery, the Eagle Brewery, which according to the 1881 county history was operated on East Congress Street by Andrew J. Leech from 1861 to 1876 (Blum lists the start at 1866). There's no record of what Leech brewed during those years, but the man seems to have been a serial entrepreneur. The 1877 *Michigan State Gazetteer* listed A.J. Leetch, pump manufacturer, on Congress Street. The January 12, 1883 *Ann Arbor Courier* mentioned a new "Enterprise Manufacturing Company" doing business "in the building of Andrew Leech east end of Congress street bridge." A follow-up item in the next issue reported A.J. Leetch as president of the new company, which manufactured kindling out of corncobs.

Ypsilanti brewing history, having abruptly ended in 1916, would not resume until 2006, when Matt and Rene Greff of Ann Arbor's successful Arbor Brewing Company opened the Corner Brewery near Depot Town, once again highlighting the ongoing synergy between Washtenaw County's two largest cities.

CHAPTER 5
LOCAL OPTIONS

[F]or the mob is eternally virtuous, and the only thing necessary to get it in favor
of some new and super-oppressive law is to convince it that that law will be
distasteful to the minority that it envies and hates.
—H.L. Mencken, Damn!: A Book of Calumny

Herman Hardinghaus had had enough. For years, these preaching
temperance people had waged war against spirituous liquor, but now they
wanted to put everyone out of business. It was too much to face the complete
ruin of the Northern Brewery on the turn of a single vote. All his investment
wasted, all his employees to lose their jobs, all the beer poured out on the
ground, the bottling lines ceased, the doors of his plant shuttered and he
himself perhaps to be hauled to the jailhouse. And to what purpose? So the
Detroit brewers could pick up his business and sell their beer to the citizens
of this county, while he himself was restrained from selling them his?

He did not understand the logic of these people threatening his livelihood,
nor could he even fathom why they would not embrace beer as the Germans
did. If the goal was temperance, was it not better to drink beer than indulge
in ardent spirits? Why assail the breweries, the honest saloon men and the
beer gardens providing the alternative to drunkenness and disorder? Why
focus such ire on the traditions of the Germans?

Time was short. He had to act if this local option question was to be stopped.

When most people think of the Prohibition era, they tend to think only of a brief period in the 1920s brimming with lurid tales of G-men and gangsters, flappers and molls, bootleggers and bathtub gin. But the roots of that misbegotten era go back a century before, to that time when no barn could be raised without the aid of barrels of whiskey.

Many of the early social reformers (the polite term for busybodies) sought only to get people to pledge to "temper" their intake of hard liquor. Beer drinking was generally not of great concern to them, it generally being considered a healthy drink and often even thought not to cause intoxication.

By the dawn of the twentieth century, however, the original temperance goal had morphed from trying to persuade people to not get hammered on hooch all the time into coercing everyone into forgoing all alcoholic beverages, beer included, via force of law. "Fanatic" (plus many other unflattering terms) really was not too harsh a word to describe these latter-day prohibitionists.

Ann Arbor's original Temperance Society was formed in 1828 or 1829 by Presbyterian minister William Page at a time when the movement was rapidly spreading across the country on the back of a major Protestant religious revival known as the Second Great Awakening. As noted previously, Washtenaw County's early settlers were terribly fond of their whiskey, so Reverend Page had his work cut out for him. The 1881 history unsurprisingly recorded that Page's group "met with great opposition at first" and for years enjoyed "only a very feeble support from the general community."

However, by the 1870s, after the movement had gathered steam, Ann Arbor had no fewer than nine temperance organizations, including a local branch of the Prohibition Party, the Ann Arbor Reform Club, the University Temperance Association, a chapter of the Woman's Christian Temperance Union, the University of Michigan branch of the Woman's Christian Temperance Union, the St. Thomas Society (for Catholics), the Ann Arbor High School Temperance Association, the Juvenile Temperance Union (yes, even the kiddies weren't safe) and a chapter of the Royal Templars of Temperance.

Clashes over questions of prohibition in nineteenth-century Ann Arbor often predictably revolved around "town vs. gown" issues, as growing numbers of citizens complained of widespread student drunkenness, a topic we'll postpone for the next chapter. But many battle lines also were drawn around sharp differences in ethnic and cultural attitudes toward social drinking, and beer was at the very center of the storm.

It may be a wee oversimplification to reduce Ann Arbor's skirmishes over prohibition to teetotaling Yankees on the one side and beer-loving Germans on the other, but to do so does provide a useful lens through which to view the contentious politics of the time. And, actually, it's not at all far from the truth.

Many, if not most, of the leaders in the temperance movement did come from backgrounds that today would be referred to as "WASP" (White Anglo-Saxon Protestant). They were typically from old New England and New York families and, religiously speaking, tended to be stern Baptists, Methodists or—like Ann Arbor's Reverend Page—Presbyterians. Over time, as the temperance movement began to expand and set its sights on breweries and beer, a collision course with German culture was inevitably set.

According to *Ann Arbor Observer* writer George F. Wieland, the seeds were sown early on when in 1834 a Presbyterian minister approached pastor Friedrich Schmid, founder of Ann Arbor's Zion Lutheran Church and Bethlehem United Church of Christ, about German drinking habits. The minister hoped that Schmid would preach to his flock the Presbyterian prohibition against not

Saloons would become the favorite target of prohibitionists in the nineteenth century. Nathan Drake's stood on East Huron Street in the 1860s. *Sam Sturgis Collection, Bentley Historical Library, University of Michigan.*

only alcohol but also tea and coffee. Schmid refused, replying that Christians filled with the Holy Spirit could be expected not to abuse the gifts of God, including beer. They did not require external compulsion.

The temperance movement's favorite target by the second half of the nineteenth century was the saloon, and free-wheeling Ann Arbor was awash with them—about one for every 150 residents by the middle of the 1860s. Like the brewing business before it, the town's saloon business by that time had largely been taken over by the ever-growing wave of German immigrants. Men with names like Albrecht, Goetz, Gwinner, Haas, Hangsterfer, Kettner, Kopf and Pfaff far outnumbered their Anglo counterparts like Drake, Eccles and Jones in the 1868 city directory's list of saloonkeepers.

Many popular accounts—mostly written by prohibitionists—paint all nineteenth-century saloons as wretched hives of scum and villainy. But it is not clear why the majority of those who owned and operated these establishments should have been anything other than honest businessmen trying to provide comfortable public spaces in the face of ongoing efforts to hamper their chosen means of earning a living. According to Wieland, late and longtime Ann Arborite Edith Staebler Kempf used to tell of one old-time saloon run by Charlie Behr where professors, lawyers and affluent German farmers all mingled over drinks with nary a hint of ill behavior.

Many of the town's saloons were of the "lager beer and refreshment" variety, including that run by Henry Binder. He was a German immigrant who established one of Ann Arbor's first hotels and then "made judicious investment in city property and erected many of the store buildings now on Main street," according to the Beakes county history. One of those buildings, known today as the Hutzel Building, stands on the southeast

Advertisement for Henry Binder's saloon from the 1868 Ann Arbor City Directory. *Ann Arbor District Library.*

corner of Main and Liberty Streets and was where in the 1870s Binder poured out the suds in his street-level saloon and lived with his family on the upper floors.

In 1871, a prominent university faculty member with impeccable Yankee credentials was elected mayor of Ann Arbor to advance the anti-saloon cause in the face of concerns over student drinking. Silas Douglas first came to Michigan in 1838 from his native New York, the son "of parents who were among the earliest settlers of New England," according to Beakes. He had served as dean of the medical school, founded the university's first chemistry lab and "also had charge of the erection of the university observatory, the south wing of the main hall and the early university system of water works."

One of the first things Mayor Douglas did in office was to pay a visit to the city's various saloon owners and threaten them with prosecution if they didn't start obeying the law prohibiting them from operating on Sundays. (He commanded such respect from the community that most obeyed.)

The story of how under Douglas Ann Arbor next established its first permanent police force provides amusing insight into the prevailing drinking culture of the time. Several state legislators in town on official business at the university were so appalled at "the moral tone, or lack thereof, in the city" (i.e., indifference to student drinking) that upon returning to Lansing, they wrote to Ann Arbor's city council about it. Embarrassed and fearful of legislative reprisals against the university, council members created a committee "to take into consideration the question of employing policemen" to better enforce the existing but widely ignored prohibition laws. The committee reported back in favor of creating a police department, noting:

> [We] *believe that the burden of the complaint of the Committee of the Legislature that visited us last winter was the moral tone of public sentiment in our midst, as was shown by the great number of saloons, billiard and gambling rooms and the riot and disorder that prevailed and was reported to prevail on our streets during the night and far into the morning.*

Douglas developed a saloon licensing system to fund the new police force. According to Beakes, it survived a challenge from the saloon owners in the state Supreme Court, and "the legislature adopted Dr. Douglas' plan throughout the state." Under the new license taxes imposed, many Ann Arbor saloons were forced out of business, and their number dropped significantly, from an estimated high of about eighty (in a town of 7,400 people) down to thirty-two.

The Ann Arbor police force, 1871. *Ann Arbor District Library.*

By 1877, Douglas had fallen from grace over a major financial scandal at the university, but the Yankee campaign against Ann Arbor's predominantly German saloonkeepers continued to intensify, getting nastier and more hysterical. According to Wieland, in 1881 the Woman's Christian Temperance Union circulated a flyer accusing saloonkeepers of turning their customers into raging beasts, listing thirty-seven of them by name and declaring, "Ann Arbor would be better off morally, socially, intellectually, and in every other way, if this disgustingly long list of men would every one of them die with the small-pox within the next week." Some Christians.

———

Since 1850, the state of Michigan had experimented with prohibitory laws and, up until 1875, actually had been a dry state. It was just that nobody paid much attention to the laws against alcohol. In early 1887, prohibition agitators persuaded the state legislature to approve a new amendment outlawing the manufacture and sale of alcoholic beverages, to be submitted to the state's voters for ratification in April. The measure failed narrowly, with Ann Arbor's heavily German population voting thumbs down by a ratio of ten to one.

Following the amendment's failure, the legislature next passed a law that enabled citizens in any county to petition for a vote on whether to ban "the manufacture and sale of malt, brewed or fermented, spirituous and vinous liquors" or continue to license breweries and saloons. If they couldn't get a statewide ban, perhaps the Yankee busybodies could at least impose their "salvation through legislation" program on the hapless residents of Washtenaw County.

But not if Herman Hardinghaus had anything to say about it. Getting word in January 1888 that the necessary petitions had been delivered and the county clerk was about to call a special election, the German owner of Ann Arbor's Northern Brewery immediately moved to file an injunction. He argued the local option law was unconstitutional on two technical grounds: it improperly delegated the state's legislative powers to counties and the title of the act did not spell out its true purpose—prohibition—as the constitution required.

All of Ann Arbor was abuzz over the issue. Crowds packed the courtroom the day of the hearing, standing for hours, straining to hear lawyers speak on both sides. Judge E.D. Kinne listened to the arguments from the bench and then adjourned the court until the next day, when he would issue his decision.

Prohibitionists and brewery and saloon workers alike waited anxiously to find out what the judge would decide, and it was well into the evening before they received the news. Hardinghaus and the brewers would be disappointed: Judge Kinne denied the injunction on the grounds he had no jurisdiction in the matter.

The vote was set for February 27. Passionate debate raged in the weeks leading up to it. The newspapers filled with letters from prohibitionists in other states attesting to how effective similar laws in their area were at making people moral and upright. Opponents pointed out how much money the city would lose in license taxes if prohibition passed. Still others criticized the language of the measure, arguing that the loophole allowing druggists to continue selling alcohol meant the prohibition wouldn't actually prohibit anything. One fiery letter decried how the proposal "robs people of their personal liberty, and makes a criminal out of every man who drinks a glass of beer."

Under the headline "Prohibition and Christianity: How a German American Looks at It," Emil Baur argued eloquently at length in the February 24, 1888 *Ann Arbor Argus* that prohibition is itself un-Christian:

> *According to prohibition Christ is a criminal. He made wine at the marriage of Cana...Prohibition is easier than humility, patience, obedience, and faithful love, which Christ demands of his disciples, to overcome the bad. It is also easier to preach prohibition and politics, and much more popular than to proclaim the crucified Christ.*

Because only the manufacture and sale, not the consumption, of alcohol would be banned under the proposal, the *Ypsilanti Sentinel* opined, "We shall simply have a chance to vote whether Mr. Foerster of Ypsilanti shall brew the beer drank here, or whether a Detroit man brew it."

Both the *Argus* and the *Ann Arbor Courier* also editorialized against the measure. For its part, the *Argus* pointed out that not only did the law's druggist loophole mean that a "yes" vote on prohibition was pointless, but also that the unscrupulous saloon men the law sought to suppress would continue undisturbed while

> [it] *is the law-abiding element of saloon keepers that will go out of the business. It will be the brewers of the county who will be compelled to cease purchasing grain and the whiskey makers of Kentucky and license counties who will enjoy a boom.*

The *Courier* recognized the measure's shortcomings this way:

> *Why prohibit the manufacture of beer? Is it not a legitimate business, sanctioned by Congress? If drank temperately there is no violation of*

law…The respectable Germans say in Germany it is not a disgrace to take a glass of beer, or wine, and that openly, and so say the English.

February 27 dawned cold and windy, and the special election brought out a heavy turnout of people, some of them traveling miles, eager to cast their ballot on the question. In the end, "it was a cold day for local optionists," in the words of the March 2 *Argus*. Prohibition failed by a wide margin: 59 percent of Washtenaw County voters said no. Predominantly German areas like Manchester, Freedom Township and, of course, Ann Arbor voted against (in Ann Arbor, only one of the six wards—the one where the Yankees lived—voted in favor). Ypsilanti shamefully went for the measure, but only by eight votes.

The *Argus* concluded that voters realized "it was not expedient to shut out the manufacture of beer in this county…or attempt to enforce a law that would not enforce." The vote made Washtenaw County the first county in the state to reject local option prohibition. Herman Hardinghaus no doubt was as pleased as he was relieved.

CHAPTER 6

THE OLD COLLEGE DRY

President Tappan showed no outward sign of his surprise. He never allowed himself to lose his composure at any time throughout the past five years—not when news first came of the war's commencement in the southern states, not when the vile editor of the *Detroit Free Press* inveighed against him incessantly in print and not when the board members began taking the power of his own office unto themselves.

But he had not expected such vindictiveness. Instead, he had keenly been looking forward to the assembly of the newly elected board of regents—all but one member different from the men he had so often clashed with—the ones presently facing him across the table to deliver their verdict. Now he would not even meet with their surely more enlightened successors.

The words still hung in the air: "...hereby removed from the office and duties of president of the University of Michigan." Tappan drew himself up into his most dignified posture and fixed his steady gaze first on Regent Brown, then Bishop, then the others, finally letting his eyes rest on Regent McIntyre, who could not countenance even a single glass of wine nor cup of beer.

"This matter belongs to history," he told them. "The pen of history is held by Almighty Justice, and I fear not the record it will make of my conduct, whether public or private, in relation to the affairs of the university."

———•———

Has there ever been a time when college students didn't consume large amounts of alcohol and engage in rambunctious behavior upsetting to their elders? In fairness to at least a few of the more level-headed temperance advocates of yesteryear, Ann Arbor was the scene of a number of "boys gone wild" moments, reaching all the way back to the days of the University of Michigan's first president, Henry Philip Tappan, who would himself ultimately fall victim to prohibitionist sentiment.

The new state constitution of 1850 required the university's board of regents to elect a president, and in 1852, it settled on Tappan, a well-regarded philosopher and academician from New York. Although he sported some serious Yankee cred, including a Doctor of Divinity degree and previous stint as a Presbyterian minister, Tappan favored the German model of education, which emphasized research in science and engineering over the prevailing English-style classical arts curriculum. He sought out faculty members based on the quality and promise of their scholarship, with the standard old-boy church affiliations taking a backseat.

His attitude toward students was also notably less paternalistic. When he arrived, most of the university's fifty-seven students slept in dormitories on the campus. To make better academic use of the dorm buildings, Tappan turned the students out and charged them with finding their own off-campus lodgings. This unheard-of move alarmed townies and others who, according to historian Samuel Beakes, thought that freeing "from inquisitorial restraint even a small horde of young men" was "a most hazardous proceeding." Tappan believed that the students were old enough to be expected to "conduct themselves as gentlemen under all circumstances," but he also expected them to take responsibility should they ever be caught breaking the law.

For a time, there were no problems, with the various "direful predictions" of student misbehavior coming to nothing, according to Beakes. But within a few years, enrollment at the university had leapt to more than four hundred, and the freedom some of these students found away from their strict teetotaling Yankee families back east got the better of them, leading to a string of beer-soaked incidents curiously christened the "Dutch War."

The trouble began one night in 1856 when Jacob Hangsterfer, proprietor of a popular student hangout on the corner of Main and Washington Streets, tossed two obnoxiously drunk students out of his establishment. Being

Henry Philip Tappan, the University of Michigan's first president (1852–63), was ousted in part by teetotalers. *Image Bank BL000938, Bentley Historical Library, University of Michigan.*

obnoxious, the students couldn't let this slight go without teaching old Hangsterfer a lesson. They returned the next night with a posse of their homies wielding knives and clubs. With cries of "revenge or beer!" the crowd demanded Hangsterfer supply all of them with free brew or else "take the consequences."

Hangsterfer told them to get lost. Instead, the students swarmed all over the joint, chasing Hangsterfer's customers into the street, shattering glass, reducing the furniture to kindling and, most terribly, smashing open keg after keg of sweet, sweet beer. The local constabulary soon arrived to break up the mêlée, but no arrests were made. That would prove to be a tactical error on the part of the authorities.

A few nights later, six student miscreants loaded up at an Alpha Nu Literary Society function at Hangsterfer's before deciding to stumble over to Henry Binder's hotel and saloon, then located north of downtown not far from where Richard Hooper would start his brewery two years later. Binder's was closed for a private German ball; unfazed, the students climbed through a window and began helping themselves to the libations. In short order, they were discovered, and five of them leaped back through the window and ran off. One student, however, was caught and held hostage by Binder and the German partygoers.

The escaped students soon returned with the requisite mob from campus and demanded the release of their compadre. Binder agreed to release him only on the condition that they pay ten dollars for the pilfered drinks. This time, the students had upgraded their weaponry from mere clubs to several large logs, which they promptly used to batter the brick walls of the hotel. The besieged Binder sicced his dog on his youthful tormentors, but they killed the overmatched pooch. Other students then arrived bearing the muskets they used in military drills and prepared to escalate the standoff. At this point, Binder backed down and released the captive beer thief, prudently putting an end to the night's hostilities.

The next morning, Binder swore out warrants with the police for the arrest of six students he had been able to identify. They retaliated by threatening to remind the cops of an old charge against the saloonkeeper for selling alcohol to minors. He quickly withdrew the warrants.

By the 1860s, various other incidents involving drunken students, including the death of one during a fraternity initiation gone wrong, had led to an informal agreement between the city and the university that no liquor licenses would be granted to any establishments east of Division Street, creating a "dry line" between town and campus that would last well into the 1960s.

Meanwhile, pressure on President Tappan was increasing. Although under his leadership the University of Michigan now boasted more than 650 students and enjoyed a national reputation as a premier institution of higher learning, several members of the board of regents personally disliked him. They viewed him as snooty and condescending (which he was), and worse, in the eyes of at least one teetotaling regent, he took a glass of wine with his meals and did not care if students drank beer (he only objected to their drinking hard liquor).

After years of behind-the-scenes scheming, the haters, due to be replaced following the 1863 election of a new board, made their move in a lame-duck meeting and fired the University of Michigan's visionary first president. Tappan had in the span of a decade turned an undeveloped little college of a few dozen students into a prestigious educational powerhouse equipped with scientific laboratories, extensive libraries and museums, a first-rate faculty and a curriculum covering a wide range of academic disciplines.

But hey, you know, *the students were drinking beer*.

—·—

Not all Michigan students who drank vast quantities of beer engaged in wanton violence and destruction. Some instead were named all-Americans and Rose Bowl MVPs.

Neil Worthington Snow is one of the University of Michigan's most celebrated student-athletes of yore. He was, according to the February 14, 1914 issue of the *Michigan Alumnus*, "the ideal athlete, and a man of more than

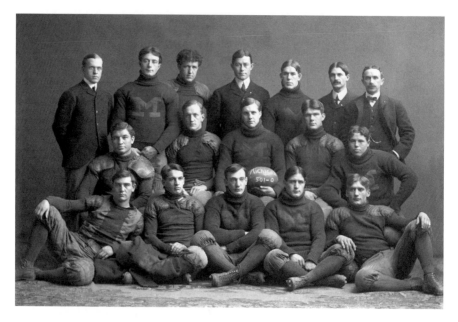

The legendary 1901 "Point-a-Minute" University of Michigan football team. Neil Snow is second from the left in the middle row. *Image Bank BL001019, Bentley Historical Library, University of Michigan.*

average ability in his classes." From 1898 to 1902, Snow collected varsity letters in sports like lesser men collect boring stuff like coins or stamps, racking up an unsurpassed total of eleven: three in track, four in baseball and four in football.

It would be on the gridiron that Snow's legend would shine brightest. As a freshman, he started every game at end for the 1898 team that went 10-0 and defeated the University of Chicago, giving Michigan its first-ever Western Conference championship and inspiring student Louis Elbel to write a little ditty known as "The Victors." He captained first-year coach Fielding Yost's nationally famous "point-a-minute" squad of 1901, which finished 11-0 and annihilated its regular season opponents by a mind-blowing combined score of 501–0. And on January 1, 1902, in the first Rose Bowl ever played, Snow ran for five touchdowns on the way to a 49–0 Michigan stomping of Stanford. (His five touchdowns still stand as a Rose Bowl record.) His performance earned him the adoration of nationally famous sportswriter Grantland Rice, as well as all-American honors, making him at the time only the second Michigan athlete to be so recognized.

Off the field, Snow kept in top shape by guzzling brewskis. To be more specific, he was a huge fan of Pale Select Beer from Detroit's Koppitz-

Neil Snow demanded beer from Detroit's Koppitz-Melchers brewery for appropriating his name for an advertisement without asking. The brewery happily delivered. *Collection of Mark Bomia.*

Melchers Brewing Company, a brewery started in 1890 by former Stroh head brewer Konrad Koppitz and another Stroh employee, Arthur Melchers.

Somehow, the brewery folks got wind of Snow's fondness for their product and, unbeknownst to him, placed an ad in the program for the June 13, 1902 baseball game between Michigan and Cornell in which they turned the all-American's thirst into an unwitting endorsement. When Snow found out that his name had been appropriated without his knowledge or consent, he did what any aggrieved college student in his position would do: he asked for free beer for himself and his buds.

Snow's letter to the brewery, sent the day of the baseball game, is too good not to quote in full:

Gentlemen:

Enclosed I send your ad which appeared in today's Michigan-Cornell official base-ball score card. I don't deny the allegation I drink Koppitz-Melchers Pale Select about as often as I can get hold of it. But there are a lot of people that didn't know it before. The sensibilities of the more unreasonably puritanical have been shocked and my reputation with them seriously impaired by this same ad. It didn't do me a bit of good. It may have done you some. If you want to make an awful hit with me and a few of my most intimate friends, and do it in a very gracious sort of way, the best way to do would be to send a case or two of that same Pale Select, express prepaid, to the address below.

Very Truly Yours,
Neil W. Snow

Just three days later, Snow received a return letter in which he was giddily informed that the ad had generated "such favorable comment" that the brewery operators were pleased to send along the requested case of beer. Drink it, they said, "as a bumper to our success." They further thanked him for "the privilege accorded us in this matter" and promised to "reciprocate at every opportunity."

Whether Snow and his friends ever received any further reciprocity from Koppitz-Melchers after draining this case of Pale Select is not known.

—--—

A little more than a month before Neil Snow polished off his free case of beer, other University of Michigan students provided a memorable welcome to one of the most famous and "unreasonably puritanical" prohibition crusaders of the day, Carrie Nation. Known as the "Vessel of Wrath," the fifty-six-year-old, twice-married daughter of an unstable woman (family tradition?) had made a national name for herself by vandalizing saloons throughout her home state of Kansas. She had been arrested time and again for smashing up bars with an axe, and to help raise money to pay her fines, she went on tours hawking souvenir photographs and hatchets and selling tickets to her speeches, which other completely misguided people apparently paid to hear.

During her May 2 whirlwind tour of Ann Arbor—during which she smashed nothing, to the relief of the city's saloonkeepers—she addressed a crowd of one thousand students from her horse-drawn carriage on the corner of State Street and North University Avenue, near the present-day Ashley's Pub. Toward the end of her speech, Nation asked how many intended to vote for prohibition in the next election. According to an account in the May 3 *Washtenaw Daily Times*, "Every mother's son in the mob put both hands high in the air" and cheered when she mentioned "the Devil."

Celebrity vandal Carrie Nation's 1902 visit to Ann Arbor did not win many converts to her cause. *Ralph Tinkham Collection, Bentley Historical Library, University of Michigan.*

The students were just beginning to have their fun with "the smasher." Next, they passed forward what appeared to be a bottle of whiskey and called loudly for her to break it. Raising the bottle over her head, Nation brought it crashing down on the carriage wheel, shattering the glass and filling the air over the street with the smell of rotten eggs. Some chemistry student with a great sense of humor had replaced the hooch with a solution of hydrogen sulfide.

"The collegians simply made a farce of the whole performance," noted the *Daily Times*, concluding its report with a description of how the students threatened to overturn Nation's carriage in a rush to grab her inventory of souvenir hatchets. She signaled her drivers to get her out of there, and the mocking throng chased the clattering carriage down the length of the block before being outdistanced and giving up.

Nation would look back fondly on her time in Ann Arbor a few years later, writing in her memoirs:

> *I have been to all the principal universities of the United States. At Cambridge, where Harvard is situated, there are no saloons allowed, but in Ann Arbor the places are thick where manhood is drugged and destroyed.*

One of the era's most beloved places for young men to get drugged and destroyed (or at least pass a few pleasant hours throwing back beers with their college mates) was Joe Parker's Famous College Saloon, which at the time of Carrie Nation's visit in 1902 stood near the northwest corner of Main and Huron Streets. In its heyday, Joe's was "known to over one hundred thousand University of Michigan men and their friends," according to DeWitt Millen, an alumnus of both institutions. In his loving recollection of the place, Millen wrote that

> *it brings back a flood of great times, many great stories, thousands of college foot-ball plots, and a number of crooked walks home, with the Ann Arbor Police Force of eight men, trying to handle five thousand young bucks, out for a good time.*

Michigan grads celebrate at the beloved Joe Parker's Saloon, which once stood on Ann Arbor's North Main Street. *Bentley Historical Library, University of Michigan.*

Regulars were greeted by Joe himself, who would call from behind the bar, "How many beers, boys?" Spilled foam and sticky mug rings covered the thousands of names carved into the wood tables where illustrious Michigan alumni sat and drank, literally making their mark. The names included those who went on to success as playwrights, musicians, lawyers, novelists and athletes, including teammates and future College Football Hall of Famers Willie Heston and Neil Snow.

According to Millen, Snow was introduced to Joe's his very first week on campus by a gang of upperclassmen aiming to teach the lanky freshman his lesson. After many beers, they followed him out of Joe's on his walk home and charged him, intending to knock him into the nearby Huron River. But in an early display of the athletic prowess that would earn him all-American recognition, Snow gave six of his assailants "a free bath above the dam." The rest of the upperclassmen retreated and allowed the freshman to continue on his way.

In 1912, the building housing Joe's Saloon was demolished to make way for a five-and-dime store, and Joe Parker relocated to the corner of North Fourth Avenue and East Ann Street, opening a new business called the Catalpa Inn, after the catalpa trees growing nearby. It included a saloon and still attracted a robust student crowd, but the adoption of statewide prohibition in 1918 killed Joe's business for good.

For a beer bar that's been gone for a century, Joe's Saloon is surprisingly still very much a part of Ann Arbor. It, along with another saloon of the time, the Orient, is immortalized in these anonymously penned verses still regularly sung by the venerable University of Michigan Men's Glee Club (a group very familiar with beer-related traditions):

I want to go back to Michigan,
To dear Ann Arbor town,
Back to Joe's and the Orient,
And back to some of the money I spent,
I want to go back to Michigan,
To dear Ann Arbor town,
I want to go back; I got to go back,
To Michigan.

Oh! Father and Mother pay all the bills,
And we have all the fun,

In the friendly rivalry of college life, Hooray!
And we have to figure a helluva lot,
To tell what we have done,
With the coin we blew at dear old Michigan!

Joe's survives in other ways as well, according to Ann Arbor historian Wystan Stevens. Pedestrians strolling past a bookstore presently situated on Fourth and Ann, in the former Catalpa Inn, can look down and see embedded in the sidewalk by the store's entrance an old mosaic spelling out the name "Joe." And those wooden tabletops carved with the names of so many famous beer-drinking Michigan alums? Some have been preserved and hang on a back wall inside the Michigan Union Grill on State Street.

Chapter 7
PROHIBITION REARS ITS UGLY HEAD

Clara Richards froze. She wasn't expecting visitors, and that meant the sound of a car in her driveway could not be anything but bad news. Peering through a crack in the drapes, she confirmed her worst fear: three cops—two Ypsilanti, one sheriff—were clambering out of a squad car and approaching the house.

Frantically, she ran into the kitchen, pulling a large jug from the cabinet. Unstopping it, she upended it into the sink and watched as its contents chugged—not fast enough for her liking—into the drain. The rough smell of evaporating alcohol practically curled her nose hairs.

She had been lucky last year when the cops pinched her partner at their old house. They wanted to stick a bootlegging charge on her, too, but didn't have the evidence. And she was determined that they would not have any this time, either.

As the last of the illicit liquid washed away, she heard the cops' voices from the yard just outside the kitchen window. Why were they not going to the front door? She dared to sneak a look through the curtain and immediately felt her wildly beating heart drop.

She had forgotten that the kitchen sink was not connected to the city water system. The policemen were standing by the drainpipe, collecting the evidence as it poured right into their hands.

Michigan governor Chase Osborn (1911–13) took aim at brewery-owned saloons, "the breeding place of vice." *Image Bank BL000396, Bentley Historical Library, University of Michigan.*

November 7, 1916, was a bitter day for beer drinkers in Michigan, and it wasn't because of the hops in their brew. The voters of the state in their infinite folly approved, 353,378 to 284,754, what the prohibitionists had been working for for so long: a constitutional ban on the manufacture and sale of alcohol. This time, even Ann Arbor—the German-dominated Second Ward excepted, of course—joined the majority in favor. The ban was to take effect on May 1, 1918, a full year and a half before national prohibition, and last "forever."

The years leading up to the vote had witnessed ever-increasing political attacks on alcohol with newer, more sophisticated groups like the Anti-Saloon League ramping up the shrill campaign against anyone, anywhere who dared to enjoy a drop of booze or beer. (It must be pointed out that the Anti-Saloon League, like the Woman's Christian Temperance Union before it, began in *Ohio.*) Already by 1916, the prohibitionists' relentless efforts had resulted in forty-five of Michigan's eighty-three counties voting themselves dry.

In 1912, the state's first and only Yooper governor, Chase Osborn, had written to the legislature asking for passage of a bill banning the latest whipping-boy of the prohibitionists, the reviled brewery-owned saloon, which he called "the breeding place of vice" and an "evil-baited man trap." Outlaw brewery-owned saloons now, he told his fellow politicians, or else

the day will soon come when the people of Michigan will rise in righteous wrath and wipe out all of the saloons by state-wide prohibition…Far down in the hearts of the people they are moral and desire that which is right and wholesome. If they can cure without fanaticism or resorting to extremes they will do so, but in time they will cure.

When the fanatics' "cure" came, 3,285 Michigan saloons, sixty-two breweries, two distillers and an unknown number of wholesalers were forced to shutter their doors.

In Ann Arbor, small prohibitionist victories had been advancing for years as well. The "dry line" informally established between the university campus and downtown in the 1860s was codified as part of the city charter in 1903 and extended east on Fuller, putting at least one popular saloonkeeper, Doc Rose, out of business. Mayor Arthur Brown complained to the city council in 1904 of "the conduct of certain liquor dealers in this city who constantly violate the law," urging—wait for it—another law to deal with them.

In 1909, Harvard-educated Yankee transplant and influential minister of Ann Arbor's First Unitarian Church Henry Wilder Foote thundered against the saloon as "a curse to the community which tolerates it, a

Men drinking beer in the barroom of the American Hotel, now the Earle Building, in downtown Ann Arbor, 1905. *Sam Sturgis Collection, Bentley Historical Library, University of Michigan.*

menace to public morality, and an enemy to the best development of the commonwealth." Even worse, the neighborhood beer joint was also "a breeding-place of disease and immorality and a constant source of corruption in municipal and state government." Probably the city's bar owners were also responsible for bad weather.

A few months later, the Ann Arbor City Council unanimously approved an ordinance imposing new costs and requirements on "saloons and all places, except drug stores, where spirituous, malt, brewed, fermented, vinous or intoxicating liquors are sold." Those who wished to apply for an annual saloon license needed to put up a $500 bond, pay a $150 fee and provide signatures from ten "reputable and respectable citizens of this city" attesting to the applicant's "good reputation, fame, and moral character." The ordinance also banned the common saloon practice of providing free lunches to customers, as well as any "gambling, dancing, sparring matches, moving pictures, or similar attractions."

Such laws often exacerbated the very issues they were to supposedly address. In *The Economics of Prohibition*, economist Mark Thornton dissects the dynamic: saloonkeepers, needing to earn more to pay the increasing costs of licenses and fees, at the same time found their businesses' hours of operation restricted and that they were legally barred from boosting their trade by offering their customers honest enticements. To make ends meet, some saloon men turned to shady practices like watering down their booze or accepting kickbacks from prostitutes and gamblers in exchange for providing a base of operations. Many saloons defied the law against closing on Sunday—often the only day their working-class customers had off—by covering their windows and bribing police and politicians to look the other way. These practices, in turn, led to more calls for raising license fees and further restricting the saloons' hours and operations, and a vicious circle was born.

Statewide and then national prohibition put an end—at least for a while—to Ann Arbor's last remaining brewery, Christian Martin and Matthias Fischer's Michigan Union. One former worker, Ernie Splitt, recalled the day in 1918 when the government enforcers showed up at the brewery on Fourth Street as the "saddest" of his life. "We stood around there—we were all drinking, even the inspectors—but the rest of the beer was poured down the drain," he said in a 1975 *Ann Arbor News* feature. To commiserate, all the members of the Ann Arbor Bartenders and Brewery Workers Union threw a farewell banquet on April 21 before going their separate ways.

On the advice of the U.S. Brewers' Association, the Michigan Union Brewery had a brief go at making nonalcoholic "near beer" as the Michigan

Members of the Ann Arbor Bartenders and Brewery Workers Union bade farewell to one another and their livelihoods in 1918 as the pall of prohibition descended. *Sam Sturgis Collection, Bentley Historical Library, University of Michigan.*

Union Beverage Company; however, then as now, fake beer was not a particularly popular product. ("The Germans wouldn't have anything to do with glorified hop water," resident Will Frey recalled in a 2007 *Ann Arbor Observer* article.) The endeavor soon folded, and an ice cream company occupied the building for the next dozen years.

Of course, the thirst for beer did not disappear simply because of legislative commandments. Ohio, despite being the birthplace of two of the most obnoxious prohibition organizations, had not yet voted itself dry, so many Michiganders headed to Toledo on beer runs. One Detroit man, German newspaper editor August Marxhausen, was busted for keeping two thousand cases of beer in his house. He ultimately wound up in the state Supreme Court, which ruled that Michigan's prohibition law did not forbid possession of alcohol and, in fact, could not be invoked to prevent anyone from bringing alcohol into the state.

The decision curtailed state police roadblocks and warrantless searches at the Ohio border, which, according to *Ann Arbor Observer* writer George F. Wieland, turned violent when cops fired on cars that attempted to circumvent them. In response to the court's ruling, Governor Albert

Sleeper threatened to declare "limited martial law" but backed down in the face of further legal challenges.

The Michigan experience was only a prelude for what would happen when prohibition was imposed nationally in 1920 following ratification of the Eighteenth Amendment and passage of its enabling legislation, the Volstead Act. People's desire for alcoholic beverages naturally persisted and began to be met in alternative ways, some of them famously not so savory. Bootlegging outfits and smuggling networks sprang up to take advantage of the huge profit opportunities, and they developed ever more sophisticated ways to outwit the federal, state and local "G-men," including, of course, the tried-and-true method of the payoff.

One obvious source for beer and booze was nearby Ontario, Canada, where the manufacture and export of alcoholic beverages was still perfectly legal. The Detroit River became a major smuggling hub as rumrunners

An early lesson in the futility of government prohibition, courtesy of *Detroit Times* editorial cartoonist Percy Cromwell. *Image Bank BL000401, Bentley Historical Library, University of Michigan.*

easily crossed it (even driving across the frozen water in the winter) to pick up their share of the 900,000 cases of hooch amassed in Windsor, Ontario, in just the first seven months of American dryness. Estimates note that 75 percent of all booze smuggled into the United States throughout the Prohibition era passed through the "Windsor-Detroit Funnel." A good part of this contraband served Detroit's estimated sixteen thousand to twenty-five thousand speakeasies; most of the rest passed through Washtenaw County on its way to Chicago and other points west.

Another source of beer for thirsty Ann Arborites was to just make it at home. Although there aren't conveniently precise historical records to document it, there is plenty of evidence to show that homebrewing was a common activity during the prohibition years. Many families turned to products like Stroh's best-selling "hopped malt syrup," officially sold "for baking, confectionary or beverage use," but according to Peter Blum, "everyone knew it was for brewing."

A front-page story in the June 2, 1919 *Daily Times News* asking, "Have You a Little Brewery at Home?" described homebrewing in Ann Arbor as "an every day occurrence." The story allowed that the result was "not always as palatable" as that brewed by the recently departed Michigan Union brewery, but that "anybody of an inquiring turn of mind" could easily get recipes, ingredients and information "which will allow him to brew beer at home." Amusingly, the story also spoke of "packages of powder" that were rumored to instantly produce beer when mixed with water but added that Ann Arborites preferred to actually brew their own.

The homebrewing story went on to opine that illegal distilling "doubtless" also occurred in Ann Arbor. As if to underscore this, another article on the same page detailed a "wild chase" and shootout in which crooked former Detroit cop Clayton Placeway was eventually apprehended near State and Huron Streets by Ann Arbor's finest for transporting 180 quarts of whiskey and 108 quarts of gin.

Other area moonshiners were hard at work producing for the local markets. According to a report in the January 3, 1920 *Daily Ypsilanti Press* cited by historian James Thomas Mann, Washtenaw deputy sheriff Dick Elliott received a tip about an illegal distillery operating on a farm three miles outside Ypsilanti. When he and two deputies raided the farmhouse on New Year's Day, they found a twenty-gallon copper still, fourteen barrels of corn and raisin mash and a bottling works. The men behind the operation, Sam Dromby and Eli Dometri, were nowhere to be found—they had been pinched earlier on their way to Detroit toting a trailer load of contraband for sale.

Ann Arbor bootleggers, date unknown. *Sam Sturgis Collection, Bentley Historical Library, University of Michigan.*

Newspapers in the ensuing years are rife with stories of alcohol busts. The December 23, 1921 *Ann Arbor Times News* reported how a combined force of Ypsilanti, Ann Arbor and state police raided two Ypsilanti blind pigs, arresting four men and seizing 103 pints of beer, four quarts of whiskey and a half-gallon of wine. Under the subhead "Paroled Bootlegger Taken Again; Sheriff Captures Load of Beer," the December 11, 1922 *Times News* reported that forty-year-old Ann Arbor resident Pete Kallas of 120 North Fourth Avenue had been picked up for his second bootlegging offense and that Leo Kohler of Wyandotte, a Detroit suburb directly across the river from Canada, got nailed driving a carful of brews.

In her book *Tales from the Ypsilanti Archives*, historian Laura Bien related the story of the 1923 arrest of "flapper bootlegger" Clara Richards. Richards was too old to be a real flapper—the fashionable young women who smoked, drank and wore short skirts—but the forty-year-old nevertheless wore her hair in a flapper-style bob as she conducted her illegal business. At first, she partnered with another Ypsilantian, Byron Tanner, whose North

Huron Street secondhand store was a front for their bootlegging operation. Richards lived with Tanner and listed her occupation as "housekeeper," and when the cops busted Tanner, they were unable to link her to the bootlegging. But a few months later, after she moved to a house on Monroe Street to carry on the business, police paid her a visit, nabbing her as she tried to pour out the moonshine before they could conduct a search.

Those scofflaws who managed to evade the police and thus the headlines obviously tended not to leave behind much to attest to their doings. Consequently, nothing specific is known about the blind pigs and speakeasies of Ann Arbor's officially dry years—except that they did exist.

Renovator Max Cope discovered evidence of one such establishment, including a mechanism to clandestinely lift kegs into a secret space, on an upper floor of the building located behind the Embassy Hotel off South Fourth Avenue.

Jim Wanty, president of local family-owned beer distributor O&W, remembered his great-grandfather falling silent whenever the family asked him if he illegally brewed or served beer in the basement of his West Liberty Street bar, which in the 1920s operated in the space now occupied by the Old Town Tavern. "We don't know whether he did or not, but he definitely kept mum about it," said Wanty. "He took his secrets to the grave."

Former Grizzly Peak Brewing Company partner Barry Seifer originally wanted to open a bar called the Speakeasy on West Washington Street—where the present-day Café Zola is—because, according to former employee Karl Dickinson, that space used to house an illegal drinking spot.

Wystan Stevens told of one speakeasy in the back room of a building up in Whitmore Lake, a popular weekend destination for the wild and carefree University of Michigan students of the 1920s. Speeding around in shiny new cars given to them by mummy and daddy, many students went for beer runs that often ended badly. Historian Mann cited an item in the February 8, 1923 *Daily Ypsilanti Press* that reported the arrest of five Michigan students after they crashed their car into a fire hydrant in the wee hours. The arresting officers discovered sixty-three pints of beer in the car, which the driver said he purchased in Wyandotte on behalf of the Sigma Alpha Epsilon fraternity. The students couldn't pay their $2,000 bail and got tossed in the clink.

They were luckier than other joyriders. According to historian James Tobin, three booze-addled students died in fatal crashes on the roads outside Ann Arbor in the 1924–25 school year and four the following year, leading to the unpopular decision of the University of Michigan regents to prohibit students from driving altogether.

But this was the Roaring Twenties, the Jazz Age, the time of Scott and Zelda Fitzgerald. If students couldn't go to the party, the party would come to them.

"Bootlegger!"

Phi Kappa Sigma pledge Edmund Love was used to hearing the voice call up the stairs at the fraternity house every Friday afternoon. The weekly ritual amused him, as his brothers excitedly rushed down to the landing by the fire escape to greet the seedy-looking guy with the sacks full of illegal beer and liquor, mostly procured from Canada and distributed clandestinely to fraternities throughout Ann Arbor.

Love didn't drink himself, having come down to the university in 1930 from an area outside Flint that was dry long before "regular" prohibition. But the more cosmopolitan atmosphere of the college town—"a wet island in the midst of a dry sea"—had quietly eroded any disapproval he may have harbored toward others who liked to bend the elbow. Despite what the law said, anyone who wanted a drink could, and did, have one. It was just a matter of getting in touch with the right people, like the seedy-looking delivery guy.

Years after he had achieved fame and fortune from his 1957 book *Subways Are for Sleeping* and its subsequent adaptation as a Broadway musical, Love recalled in his memoir a particular telephone call he took in the early hours of February 11, 1931.

"For God's sake," the panicked voice on the other end of the line gasped. "If you've got any liquor in the house, get rid of it! The federals are in town, and they're raiding the fraternities!"

Love and seven of his brothers had been alone in the house playing a late-night card game. The rest of the seventy-some fraternity members had left town following the end of winter exams, but not before laying in a supply of bootlegged alcohol for the upcoming J-Hop, a three-day weekend of parties and dances. Love knew that the desks, closets and bureaus in the bedrooms upstairs were stocked full of this booze. Rather than flee, he and his fellow card-players broke into each bedroom, rifling through the personal things of their frat brothers in search of any and all alcohol. They worked for several hours, pouring out bottle after bottle and dumping the empties in the trash bins of a nearby sorority house. By the time they were done, at about six o'clock in the morning, according to Love, some thirty-seven quarts of spirits, four quarts of wine, five bottles of sparkling wine, a jug of cider and two cases of beer had been chugged down the drain.

Only an hour later, the police raid party banged on the door. Love remembered how unhappy the cops were when they found nothing but evidence that the Phi Kappa Sigma brothers had been tipped off. Later, Love learned where the heroic warning had come from: a freshman at the Delta Kappa Epsilon house, who evaded arrest by hiding in a laundry hamper when the cops stormed in, rang up Love and other fraternities once the coast was clear.

According to James Tobin, when the dust settled, seventy-five quarts of "Scotch and rye whiskey, gin, wines, bottled cocktails, imported vermouth,

"WHY? *You're a menace to society; that's* WHY!"

From the March 1931 *Gargoyle. Bentley Historical Library, University of Michigan.*

and rare cordials" were seized, and seventy-nine fraternity brothers from five houses were charged with disorderly conduct. The university ordered the houses in question shuttered for the rest of the year, evicting some two hundred frat members and rendering many cooks, porters and dishwashers jobless in the depths of the Great Depression. Prosecutors deemed that punishment good enough and dropped the charges against the brothers, but Love's seedy-looking delivery guy, revealed to be bootlegger Joe Looney, wound up in the slammer.

Reactions to the "Great Raid of 1931," as it came to be called, were fierce on both sides. University of Michigan president Alexander Ruthven praised and defended the action, while Ann Arbor mayor Edward Staebler condemned it as too harsh. The raid made national news, and hundreds of letters poured in from alumni around the country weighing in on the matter.

Oreon Scott, partner in an insurance and loan company, wrote from St. Louis to express his support for the raid, opining that "the great majority" of alumni "believe in the enforcement of the law" to protect the reputation of the university. A letter from Oakland County realtor Carl Bradt criticized the raid as "terribly drastic and certainly most unfair," considering alcohol "could be found in at least fifty percent of the homes in Ann Arbor," including those of some professors.

Student reaction was also mixed, with some affecting indifference but others willing to publicly express their disgust. Under the editorship of senior Paul Showers—future *New York Times* writer and children's book author—the campus humor magazine *Gargoyle* devoted most of the March issue to lampooning the raids. A series of cartoons portrayed a policeman busting people sleeping, praying and playing chess for "disorderly conduct" before concluding, "Aw—to hell with prohibition." Satirical articles purported to chronicle the simultaneous raid on the "Gramma Eta Yam" sorority and explained the rules for a new game called "Getting Evidence" in which players (aka cops) receive points for busting into random fraternities, scooping up all the booze and drinking it themselves.

That the law was a joke was well understood among a public weary by the 1930s of prohibition's negative effects, including increased crime, greater government corruption and intrusiveness and, worst of all, libations with serious quality control issues. Opinion had finally and overwhelmingly turned against the great Yankee busybody crusade. When ordinary Ann Arborites like Bill Metzger of Metzger's German Restaurant could be severely punished for innocently selling juice that had fermented while gangsters freely amassed fortunes with which to bribe public officials, it was time for a change.

PART II

MOVING ON

CHAPTER 8

NOISY CROWDS RECEIVE BREW

So, we have decided to give up prohibition. We have decided to go back and try personal liberty once more, the personal liberty we had before prohibition.
—Michigan governor William Comstock, April 10, 1933

On April 7, 1933, American beer drinkers could enjoy for the first time in nearly fourteen years beer that wasn't homebrewed, smuggled from Canada or produced mysteriously behind closed doors in a secluded plant located in parts unknown. At the stroke of midnight, the federal Cullen-Harrison Act—allowing for the production and sale (and, of course, heavy taxation) of 3.2 percent alcohol-by-weight beer, wine and fruit juice—took effect. Breweries that managed to survive the Prohibition era by producing de-alcoholized "near beer" had been gearing up for months and were ready.

Also ready were thirsty people in the nineteen states that did not still have to contend with their own laws banning alcohol. Under the headline "Noisy Crowds Receive Brew," an Associated Press story in that day's edition of the *Ann Arbor Daily News* told of the beer bashes in New York, Oregon, California, Minnesota, Illinois, Wisconsin—even freaking Ohio and Indiana. Brewery executives estimated that more than 1 million gallons of beer were guzzled on "New Beer's Day."

Ann Arborites had to stick with their homebrew for a little while longer: although a fall referendum had repealed the Michigan constitution's prohibition amendment, the legislature did not pass a 3.2 percent beer law until April 27. In the meantime, the Wolverine State became—by a

The Court Tavern on East Huron Street was among the first Ann Arbor establishments to serve legal beer on May 11, 1933, following the end of prohibition. *From an April 1966 edition of the* Ann Arbor News. *All rights reserved. Reprinted with permission.*

convention vote of ninenty-nine to one—the first to ratify the total repeal of the now-despised Eighteenth Amendment.

Legal beer sales in Ann Arbor resumed at 6:00 p.m. the evening of May 11, when the new beer law took effect. According to historian Grace Shackman, the Court Tavern, which stood at 108 East Huron Street, was one of twenty local establishments pouring out the suds that night.

"Men, women—everyone was out celebrating that beer came back, that Prohibition was over," Sam Sekaros recalled in Shackman's 1996 *Ann Arbor Observer* article. Gust Sekaros, Sam's father and then owner of the Court Tavern, borrowed $500 to purchase a supply of beer, which sold for fifteen cents per glass—until the busy tavern ran out at 11:00 p.m. In the morning, Gust was so flush from the night's business that he returned to the bank and repaid the loan.

According to Shackman, cars crowded the parking lots of local grocery stores to load up on cases of beer. Other establishments, like the Allenel Hotel on Fourth and Huron and the Elks Club and Preketes Beer Garden on Main Street, filled with students (who eagerly crossed the Division Street "dry line") and townies alike, all determined to make this Thursday night one of utmost festivity. Ann Arbor's noisy crowds had at last received some brew of their own.

Twenty-two Michigan breweries were initially approved by the state's newly created Liquor Control Commission to produce and sell beer. More would soon follow, including two former breweries in Ypsilanti and Ann Arbor.

On December 5, 1933, Utah became the thirty-sixth state to ratify repeal of the Eighteenth Amendment, officially ending the federal prohibition of alcoholic beverages. Each state created its own legal environment for the sale of beer, wine and booze, with most adopting the so-called three-tier approach mandating a separation between producers, distributors and retailers that

Fred Dupper tends the taps at his neighborhood watering hole, which stood where the Bach Elementary School playground now is. *Louis Velker/Ann Arbor District Library.*

survives today. Some states, like Michigan, opted to become "control" states, meaning the state would operate all or part of the distributor tier and even, in wackier places like Pennsylvania, the retail tier. (In Michigan, the state fixes prices and serves as the sole wholesaler for distilled spirits, while the beer and wine distribution system is tightly regulated but privately run.)

Prior to prohibition, breweries could and did sell directly to consumers. Many in Ann Arbor's German community picked up their beer right from the brewery and brought it home (or to their worksites) in buckets. On Saturday mornings, the Michigan Union brewery dropped off kegs (three dollars per half-barrel) at Ann Arbor's saloons and German social clubs, the latter of which were not legally obligated to close on Sundays like the former were. Club members paid fifteen cents for a ticket entitling them to five glasses of beer.

Distributors, such as Fred Dupper, also sold beers from out-of-town breweries. In 1907, Dupper inherited his father's small bar and distributorship that operated from the family's Old West Side home, not far from the Michigan Union brewery. Bottles and kegs of Green Seal and other brands from Toledo's Buckeye Brewing Company came into town via the Ann Arbor Railroad, were unloaded at the Ashley Street depot and then transported by horse-drawn wagon to Dupper's house. He then delivered the beer to stores, saloons, restaurants, fraternities and even private residences. According to Shackman, more than a few Ann Arbor beer drinkers disloyally claimed that the Toledo brews tasted better than the local product.

Following prohibition, many distributors, eager to take advantage of the pent-up thirst for beer, applied for licenses under the new three-tier system. Among them was O&W (Liquor Control License No. 007), which actually traces its roots back to 1915. Saloonkeeper William Seagert, who ran the Union Bar on Ann Arbor's West Liberty Street, where the Old Town Tavern is today, used to make regular beer (and, during prohibition, "near beer") runs to the Stroh brewery in Detroit. Eventually, he began taking orders from, and delivering Stroh beverages to, other saloons around town. After prohibition, the distributorship passed to Seagert's son-in-law, James O'Kane, who in turn was joined by his son-in-law, Hugh Wanty. They distributed a variety of beers from their original warehouse near the corner of William and Main Streets before building a bigger and more modern one out on Jackson Road.

According to Hugh's son, Jim, who runs O&W today from its present location in Ypsilanti with his brother, Doug, Ann Arbor had seven different beer distributors in the years following the establishment of the three-

Following prohibition, as many as seven beer distributors operated in Ann Arbor. *From a 1939 edition of the* Ann Arbor News. *All rights reserved. Reprinted with permission.*

tier system. Postwar consolidation and other changes in the beer business eventually eliminated most of these early distributorships, which tended to concentrate on beers from regional breweries like Stroh, Pfeiffer and Schlitz.

But local beer also made a comeback following the repeal of prohibition. According to Shackman, sometime in 1933, three local contractors—Chris Mack, Stanley Thomas and Ed Bliska—resurrected the old Michigan Union brewery, rechristening it the A.A. Brewing Company and, later, Ann Arbor Brewing Company. They hired Jake Ludwig, a former brewer who had turned to farming during prohibition, to oversee the operation. The lager brewery was refitted with new equipment, including a modern bottling line that didn't always work smoothly. Will Frey, who worked at the brewery beginning in 1937, recalled having to move bottles by hand into cases for shipping. "There was a fair amount of broken glass in the brewery, but we also got pretty good at it," he told Shackman in a 2007 *Ann Arbor Observer* feature. "You learned fast, or you'd get all bloody."

The newfangled Ann Arbor Brewing was "optimistically" rated at a capacity of fifty thousand barrels, according to Peter Blum. Throughout the

Hugh Wanty of longtime local Miller distributor O&W recognized Ann Arbor's thirst for "different" beers like Heineken in the 1980s. *From a June 1989 edition of the* Ann Arbor News. *All rights reserved. Reprinted with permission.*

years, it produced and sold a number of beers, or at least brands. Bottles of Cream Top Old Style Beer, Ann Arbor Old-Tyme Beer and Town Club Beer ("It's tops!") were cracked and poured throughout Ann Arbor, Manchester, Milan and other German-heavy area towns. According to Frey, shipments even went farther afield, including to an Amish population in Ohio and a group of German farmers in Texas.

Hops were shipped in from somewhere out west, and the malt came from a Chicago grain dealer, Frey remembered, but the brands were actually all the same beer—only the labels that he and the other bottlers attached were different. "We'd start with, say, six hundred of Old Tyme, then three hundred of Town Club," he told Shackman. Mary Hunt's 1975 *Ann Arbor News* feature on the brewery noted that this mix-and-match labeling didn't occur just inside the brewery walls. One resident, she said, remembered seeing cases of unlabeled beer in the refrigerator of a local bar with boxes of gummed labels nearby so the bartender could slap whichever one the customer ordered onto the bottle before serving it.

The brewery did make at least one beer that was different: Ann Arbor Old-Tyme Bock Beer, a stronger, maltier lager that, true to German style

Workers bottling beer at the Ann Arbor Brewing Company, the city's only post-prohibition brewery. *From the August 7, 1936* Ann Arbor News. *All rights reserved. Reprinted with permission.*

and tradition, came out every spring. But whether they caught on to the disingenuous attempts at branding or not, at least some Ann Arborites seemed not to particularly prefer the local product. Jim Wanty recalled his grandfather having been unimpressed. One resident quoted by Shackman pronounced, "It was considered good only for putting out fires." Former *Ann Arbor News* photography chief Eck Stanger insisted to Hunt that "Ann Arbor people didn't drink it."

But some certainly did, at least when it was free. A number of Old West Side old-timers reminisced about going through an always-unlocked door off the loading dock that led to a backroom where, according to Frey, leaky barrels that couldn't be sold were placed. Anyone who knew about the "free beer room" was welcome to stop in, pull a mug from the wall and enjoy a couple brews gratis. No one ever overindulged, resident Kurt Neumann told Hunt; they would only draw off a beer or two, sit down on barrels, talk a while and then rinse out and return their mugs.

Ann Arbor Brewing's beers must have found a customer base somewhere, however, because the brewery stayed afloat, surviving some big personnel changes beginning with the arrival of German-trained Albert Bek, who took over as brewmaster in 1938. According to Blum, Bek came to Ann Arbor following a stint at Hudepohl Brewing in Cincinnati and became a "one-man technical staff," serving not just as brewmaster but also chemist and bottle shop superintendent.

Other changes followed. A year later, a group of Chicago investors bought out the brewery's original owners and installed Charles Ackerman as president, treasurer and general manager. When the United States entered World War II in 1942, rationing played havoc with the beer business, as it did with life in general, creating numerous challenges in procuring equipment, ingredients and manpower. Nevertheless, a few changes in brewmasters later, Ann Arbor Brewing emerged at the end of the war still hanging on.

By 1947, however, postwar competition from Pabst, Stroh, Goebel and other large regionals had begun to really put the squeeze on local breweries like Ann Arbor Brewing. According to Blum, the Ackerman team managed to exit gracefully by selling out to investors Milton and Cerna Johnson. Milton took over as jack-of-all-trades, becoming president, treasurer, general manager, purchasing agent and sales and advertising manager. He engaged

The former brewery at 416 Fourth Street as it appears today. *Photo by David Bardallis.*

Fred Heusel to oversee brewery operations, and the brewery even added a new brand, Van Dyke Beer.

It wasn't enough to keep the business going, and in 1949, Ann Arbor Brewing was closed for good and the equipment sold off. In the ensuing decades, continuing industry consolidation dramatically reduced the number of breweries in the United States to just a handful of regionals and large national conglomerates, leading to the dark days when consumer choices were severely limited and American beer was the butt of many jokes. There would be no beer brewed commercially in Ann Arbor for the next forty-six years.

The neighboring Argus camera company purchased the brewery building and occupied it until the mid-1960s, when the University of Michigan acquired it and turned it into a film library and audiovisual education center. Today, it is home to the offices of *Mathematical Reviews*, the journal of the American Mathematical Society, where managing editor and beer lover Norm Richert maintains a small breweriana display. His collection includes labels, bottles and a heavy cardboard Cream Top case. The break room is adorned by one of the few beer barrels—marked "A.A. Brewing Co. Ann Arbor, Mich."—to survive the demolition of an old outbuilding. According to Richert, all but one or two of the other barrels stored there were chopped up and used for firewood. All that otherwise remains of the building's brewing past is a large vaulted cellar of fieldstone and brick, once filled with beer but now sitting dark, empty and unused.

Longtime resident and homebrewer Jeff Renner recalled a funny anecdote he heard in the 1960s from the late Brymer Williams, a beloved professor of chemical engineering at the University of Michigan who had some association with Ann Arbor Brewing. Williams, said Renner, told of the brewery's battles with the city over sewage fees, which were charged based on total water consumption. The brewery argued that it shouldn't have to pay for the water that ended up bottled as beer. The city countered that it ultimately ended up in the sewers, too, after being filtered through local beer drinkers. "Finally, a compromise was reached," Renner said. "The brewery was not charged for the water in beer that was sold *outside* of the city."

Local brewing also resumed in Ypsilanti after prohibition, but the new ventures were shorter-lived and less successful than their Ann Arbor counterparts. The former Foerster brewery on Grove Street first reopened in 1933 as Liberty Brewing Company but changed hands within a year when Christopher Vogt bought the business and renamed it the Ypsilanti Brewing Company. Vogt modernized the operation with new machinery and also purchased a few trucks to haul kegs and bottles. According to Blum, by 1936, sales of Old Ypsilanti lager totaled 16,300 barrels.

Christopher Vogt prepares to sell his "Old Ypsilanti Beer" following prohibition. *Ypsilanti Historical Society.*

Again, the growing clout of the regionals plus the changing drinking habits of the public made it hard for a local brew like Old Ypsilanti to find a market. Perhaps to emphasize his lager's bona fides among all the Strohs, Schlitzes, Blatzes and Pabsts out there, Vogt changed the beer's name to Vogt German (Style) Lager Beer. Sales remained flat or declined, and in 1941, he sold the brewery to a group of Detroit investors.

The new owners renamed the business Dawes Brewing Company. Blum speculates that the name was a gimmick designed to make their beer, Dawes Premium Draft, sound like an "exotic" Canadian import. The age of modern marketing had arrived. At any rate, their timing could not have been worse, as the advent of World War II rationing and market disruptions put the final nail in the coffin. According to Blum, the brewery shut its doors in 1943, selling most of its equipment to Detroit's Altes Brewing Company and ending Ypsilanti's local brewing scene for the remainder of the twentieth century. The building was converted to a variety of uses, including apartments, before eventually being bulldozed to make way for a redevelopment project.

Chapter 9
BEER AND CULTURE IN ANN ARBOR

For thousands of years, beer has been a vital part of human civilization. In fact, some archaeologists and historians argue that beer is actually *responsible* for human civilization, citing evidence that ancient man first formed settlements and began to cultivate crops for purposes of producing grains with which to make beer-like fermented beverages.

Whatever the truth of those claims, beer has certainly played an important role throughout Ann Arbor's own cultural history, a history so rich that it belies the city's relatively small size. From physicians and poets to professors, performers and political activists, Ann Arbor's past teems with the names, both familiar and forgotten, of people who left their imprint on the larger world in a wide variety of ways. And winding like a foamy golden river through all this human drama and endeavor is none other than that old alleged parent of civilization itself.

Few outside of Ann Arbor history buffs are likely to recognize the name A.W. Chase, but in the latter half of the nineteenth century, his phenomenally best-selling series of books graced the shelves of homes throughout the country and, indeed, even the world.

Alvan Wood Chase was born in 1817 in New York State. He left his father's farm as a teenager, traveling west and earning a living as a peddler of groceries and household "medicines" throughout Ohio and then Detroit. In 1856, as he approached age forty, Chase arrived in Ann Arbor with his wife and children in tow. He had decided that it would be a good idea to finally "qualify himself for the work he was undertaking" with a degree from the University of Michigan, whose academic reputation under president Henry Tappan had begun to spread.

This goal he failed to achieve, since, according to historian Grace Shackman, the unschooled Chase didn't know Latin, which was required to complete the university's medical program. He audited several classes at Michigan, including some with chemistry professor and future mayor Silas Douglas, but to earn the title of "doctor," he had to leave town for four months to attend the Eclectic Medical Institute of Cincinnati, which specialized in herbal medicines. If this makes him sound like a quack today, it must be remembered that respectable medical opinion of the time was in favor of such "cures" as bloodletting and mercury poisoning, which Chase to his credit recognized as the real quackery.

Ann Arbor doctor A.W. Chase's nineteenth-century home remedy books included beer recipes and were international bestsellers. *Ann Arbor District Library.*

In 1857, the newly minted Dr. Chase returned to Ann Arbor, where he continued selling various cures and treatments and compiling the numerous household recipes that he had acquired from his years of travels. These he published in increasingly voluminous versions of what would become his signature work, *Dr. Chase's Recipes, or Information for Everybody.* By 1864, he had amassed enough money to begin construction on a handsome new "publication office and book bindery" in downtown Ann Arbor where he could crank out more and better editions of his book to meet growing demand. At the time, it was the largest such facility in the Midwest.

The next year, Chase purchased a local newspaper, renaming it the *Peninsular Courier and Family*

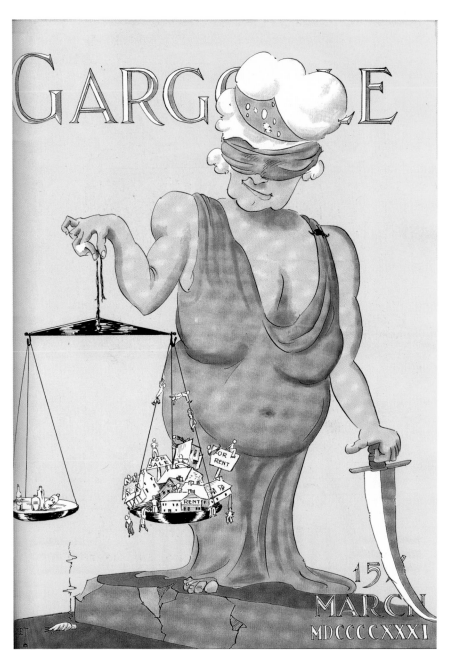

The entire March 1931 issue of the *Gargoyle* was devoted to lampooning the recent police raid of University of Michigan fraternities for possession of bootlegged liquor and beer. *Bentley Historical Library, University of Michigan.*

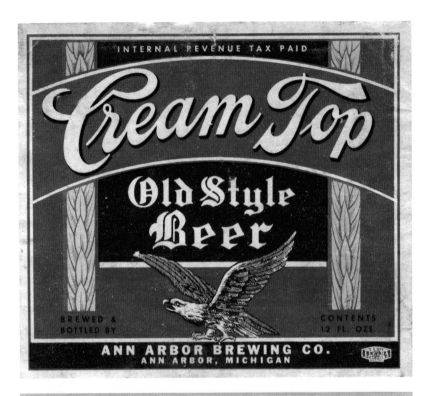

INTERNAL REVENUE TAX PAID

Cream Top

Old Style Beer

BREWED &
BOTTLED BY

CONTENTS
12 FL. OZS.

ANN ARBOR BREWING CO.
ANN ARBOR, MICHIGAN

CONTENTS
12 FLUID
OUNCES

INTERNAL
REVENUE
TAX PAID

Ann Arbor
OLD-TYME
BEER

Brewed and

Bottled by

ANN ARBOR BREWING CO., ANN ARBOR, MICHIGAN

Christopher Vogt revived the old Foerster brewery in 1934 under the name Ypsilanti Brewing Company. *Brian Stechschulte.*

Opposite: Labels from two of the post-prohibition Ann Arbor Brewing Company brands, which were said to be the same beer. *Brian Stechschulte.*

Bill Zolkowski serves up Michigan craft brews every summer at Bill's Beer Garden in downtown Ann Arbor. *Photo by Nicole Rupersburg.*

Fabled in song, Ann Arbor saloonkeeper Joe Parker also lives on in this sidewalk mosaic at the corner of Ann Street and Fourth Avenue. *Photo by Nicole Rupersburg.*

Opposite: Years after the event, concert organizer Robert Jr Whitall commissioned a new poster to commemorate the infamous 1974 "Bob Seger Barn Dance," which ended in a police raid and forty kegs of beer being dumped into Ford Lake. *Robert Jr Whitall.*

Advertisement for Ypsilanti's L.Z. Foerster Brewing Company, perhaps part of a promotional calendar. *Ypsilanti Historical Society.*

Rene and Matt Greff enjoy a little something from the beer cellar at Arbor Brewing Company. *Photo by David Bardallis.*

Laurie and Ron Jeffries at the Jolly Pumpkin brewery in Dexter. *Photo by David Bardallis.*

Once the place where beer aged in barrels, the cellar at 1327 Jones Drive now houses office space for technology startups. *Photo by David Bardallis.*

The house where Western Brewery founder Peter Brehm shot himself still stands at 326 West Liberty. *Photo by Nicole Rupersburg.*

Three of the post-prohibition Ann Arbor Brewing Company beers reunited in the former brewery building on Fourth Street. *Collection of Norm Richert. Photo by David Bardallis.*

Arbor Brewing Company head brewer Mike Moroney hard at work. *Photo by Allen Williams.*

Grizzly Peak and Blue Tractor partner Jon Carlson. *Photo by Allen Williams.*

Head brewer Oliver Roberts, with assistant brewers Rick Wilson and Karl Hinbern, at the Wolverine State Brewing brewhouse. *Photo by Allen Williams.*

Grizzly Peak head brewer Duncan Williams in the brewhouse. *Photo by Allen Williams.*

Blue Tractor head brewer Tim Schmidt. *Photo by Allen Williams.*

The Jolly Pumpkin Café in downtown Ann Arbor. *Photo by Allen Williams.*

The ivy-covered former Central Brewery, now an apartment building, at the corner of North Fifth Avenue and Summit Street. *Photo by Allen Williams.*

Contract-brewed Frog Island beer briefly enjoyed its own space before being shut down by the City of Ypsilanti. *Photo by Allen Williams.*

Chris Martinson opened the Chelsea Alehouse Brewery in 2013, thirty years after Ted Badgerow closed the Real Ale Company. *Photo by David Bardallis.*

Mugs awaiting club members at the Corner Brewery in Ypsilanti. *Photo by Allen Williams.*

Opposite, top: After years of confusing consumers, Jolly Pumpkin finally began brewing a pumpkin beer, La Parcela, in 2008. *Photo by David Bardallis.*

Opposite, middle: The annual Michigan Brewers Guild Summer Beer Festival brings thousands of Michigan craft beer lovers to the Ann Arbor/Ypsilanti area every July. *Photo by David Bardallis.*

Opposite, bottom: Judging beers at the annual Brews Crews homebrew competition in Ypsilanti. *Photo by David Bardallis.*

Tanks above the bar at Blue Tractor BBQ & Brewery in downtown Ann Arbor. *Photo by Allen Williams.*

Brewer Mike Bardallis mans the Grizzly Peak brew system. *Photo by Allen Williams.*

Visitant, and issued the twenty-fourth edition of *Dr. Chase's Recipes* in a hardbound version that sold for $1.25 ($2.00 with "Morocco gilt"), with a $1.00 paperback version also available. He soon turned over editorship of the newspaper to John Knight, preferring to focus his full attention on his exploding book business.

The 1865 edition of the book included about eight hundred recipes for everything from molasses candy and oyster soup to dropsy syrup, dyspeptic tea and "toad ointment," which awesomely included boiled toads as an ingredient. The book also promised to provide "a rational treatment of pleurisy, inflammation of the lungs, and other inflammatory diseases" and help with "general female debility and irregularities." But most importantly, the book's twenty-four-page "Saloon Department" advised that

> [if] *saloon keepers, and grocers, who deal in wine, beer, cider, &c., will follow our directions here, and make some of the following articles, they, and their customers, will be better pleased than by purchasing the spurious articles of the day; and families will find them equally applicable to their own use.*

The "articles," at least as far as varieties of beer were concerned, included "Spruce, or Aromatic Beer"; lemon beer; ginger beer; "Philadelphia" beer; "Patent Gas" beer; "Corn Beer, Without Yeast"; and "Strong Beer, English, Improved." The good doctor certainly had done his homework, and one likes to imagine that the perfection of these recipes provided him with hours of enjoyable research.

Or maybe not. Many of the recipes call for ingredients that sound a bit peculiar to the modern ear, such as brown sugar, cream of tartar, egg whites, allspice, cloves, lemon juice and sassafras oil. But Chase's instructions under "Ale, Home-Brewed—How It Is Made" should be recognizable to anyone familiar with the basic brewing process:

> *For this purpose a quarter of malt, (8 bus.) is obtained at the malt-house—or, if wished to be extra strong, nine bushels of malt—are taken, with hops, 12 lbs.; yeast, 5 qts.*
>
> *The malt, being crushed or ground, is mixed with 72 gals. of water at the temperature of 160°, and covered up for 3 hours, when 40 gallons are drawn off, into which the hops are put, and left to infuse. Sixty gallons of water at a temperature of 170° are then added to the malt in the mash-tub, and well mixed, and after standing 2 hours, sixty gallons are drawn off.*

The wort from these two mashes is boiled with the hops for 2 hours, and after being cooled down to 65°, is strained through a flannel bag into a fermenting tub, where it is mixed with the yeast and left to work for 24 or 30 hours. It is then run into barrels to cleanse, a few gallons being reserved for filling up the casks as the yeast works over.

Chase's book, beer recipes and all, became a massive bestseller throughout America and even internationally, eventually selling more copies than any other book save the Bible, at least according to contemporary claims. In 1869, fearing for his health under the stress of maintaining a publishing empire as well as a busy medical practice, the aging Chase sold all his business interests to local lumber baron Rice Beal, who, according to Samuel Beakes's county history, "pushed the sale of Dr. Chase's receipt books until the profits on their sales reached seventy-five thousand dollars a year."

Chase left for Minnesota to pass what few years he believed he had left. But with time and quiet to reflect, he soon realized that he was not at death's door after all and that he had made a huge mistake. Chase returned to Ann Arbor a year later and tried to resume publishing recipe books, but Beal took him to court and won a lawsuit forcing him to seek a publisher outside Michigan.

By the 1880s, now nearly penniless and alone, Chase was working on what he considered the best new edition of his recipe book yet, but he died in 1885, unable to find anyone willing to publish it. Shortly afterward, it was issued posthumously by a Detroit publisher as *Dr. Chase's Third, Last, and Complete Receipt Book and Household Physician*. Dubbed the "memorial edition," it included a preface that asserted that "Dr. Chase's name is a household word in millions of homes; we trust this book will make it a familiar name in a million more."

The rampaging prohibitionist movement ensured that the "Saloon Department" was omitted in this final edition. In fact, the only beer recipe listed was for a "strictly temperance beer" of ginger root, sassafras bark and dandelion. Even worse, the political and intellectual climate of the time apparently dictated that a "Temperance Pledge" also be inserted:

A pledge I make, no wine to take…
Nor lager beer, my heart to cheer;
Nor sparkling ale, my face to pale.

Dr. Chase's name and likeness continued to be used on various publications and products until well into the 1950s, and the building that once housed his mighty publishing empire still stands on the northwest corner of Miller Avenue and Main Street. But it's unlikely anyone still uses his recipes to make beer.

———·—

Thirty-four-year-old W.H. Auden was already well known as a practiced writer of verse when he arrived in Ann Arbor in 1941 to begin a term as visiting professor of English. The man now regarded by many critics as the greatest English poet of the twentieth century taught only two semesters at the University of Michigan, but the friendships he forged during his time in Ann Arbor left a long-lasting legacy. Plus, like any good Englishman, he enjoyed his beer.

Born in York in 1907 and educated at Christ Church, Oxford, Auden had six published volumes under his belt and, like many other writers of the 1930s, a reputation as a left-wing socialist intellectual. But his experiences traveling to places like China, Iceland and, most importantly, Spain during the Spanish Civil War had by the early 1940s coalesced to form in his mind a worldview too nuanced to be so easily pigeonholed.

Auden taught two 100-level classes, "Fate and the Individual in English Literature" and "Analysis of Poetry," which had a combined enrollment of forty-three. One of his students, Robert Chapman, remembered Auden wearing blue jeans, a plaid shirt and slippers to class. His English accent,

Poet W.H. Auden at the train station in Ann Arbor, circa 1941. *Will Hathaway.*

combined with a speech impediment, made it difficult at first for the students to understand him, but once they adapted to "the power and strangeness of his discourse," they found themselves enraptured. Auden's informal presence and method of teaching were highly unusual at the time, but Chapman noted that his style anticipated professors of the 1960s and '70s.

Auden rented a house at 1223 Pontiac Trail, built on the foundation of a previous house that, in one of those cosmic coincidences, had been occupied by another world-famous poet, Robert Frost, in the 1920s. (The Victorian Frost house was relocated to the Henry Ford Museum in Dearborn in about 1936; the modernist house Auden lived in remains.)

There he roomed with a student and friend, Charles Miller, who in his memoir, *Auden: An American Friendship*, recalled the beer and bull sessions that resulted in "armies of empties formed on the coffee table and in the kitchen." According to Miller, Auden's students came over to listen to records, smoke, drink and discuss—and sometimes argue about—literature, the war in Europe, school politics, Michigan football and even "American

The building at 122 West Washington Street first became a saloon in 1895, with Flautz's Tavern, the Del Rio and today's Grizzly Peak Den being just a few incarnations over the years. *Sam Sturgis Collection, Bentley Historical Library, University of Michigan.*

versus imported beer." Chapman remembered Auden as "delightedly expansive, pleased to have company, a gracious host," despite occasional sharp disagreements on things like Hemingway's worth as a novelist.

Auden also enjoyed occasional pub crawls around Ann Arbor. Miller recounted a time they went to Flautz's Tavern at 122 West Washington Street, later home to the legendary Del Rio bar and current home of the Grizzly Peak Brewing Company Den. The always unassuming Auden was not thrilled with the vibe, asking, "Isn't there a common place where, uh, the workers go? A kind of beer hall?"

Miller knew of such a place around the corner on Ashley Street, a "big bare 'café'" where they relocated to sit among the empty tables. When Miller tried to order a "Canadian ale," Auden slapped down his young friend's nascent beer snobbery by telling their wary waitress, "We'll have just what the others are having!" Miller named neither the café nor the beer they drank, but he did remember it was "mediocre."

Auden moved to New York following the end of spring semester 1942, but he returned to Ann Arbor less than a year later to attend the christening of a child born to Albert and Angelyn Stevens, a young academic couple to whom he had grown close. Today, Auden is most popularly remembered for such poems as "Funeral Blues," often mistakenly called by its first line, "Stop all the clocks," and "September 1, 1939," written on the occasion of the outbreak of World War II.

Some critics consider the poetry Auden published in the early 1940s to be among his best work. But one poem of the era, "Mundus et Infans," has special meaning for a certain lifelong Ann Arborite. Auden wrote it specifically for his friends Albert and Angelyn to commemorate the birth of the godson who bears his name: Wystan Auden Stevens.

———•———

Imagine if you could win a Nobel Prize in beer. Nearly twenty years after Auden left Ann Arbor, another former University of Michigan professor did just that. All right, he actually won the Nobel Prize in physics. But beer played a role in the early experiments he conducted in the work that led to his winning the prestigious award—and nearly got him fired.

Donald Glaser was like many other twenty-five-year-old collegians in 1952 Ann Arbor. He liked to go out for a beer every now and then, with his preferred destination being the Pretzel Bell on East Liberty Street. The P-Bell, as it was affectionately known, was a favorite student hangout for decades, chiefly because it was the first place to get a drink past the "dry line" of Division Street that banned bars in the area immediately surrounding campus.

But unlike many other twenty-five-year-olds, Glaser had a great idea for a device that physicists could use to better study the paths of the subatomic particles that were created whenever they smashed apart atoms. According to local legend, Glaser got the idea for what became known as the bubble chamber one night at the P-Bell by watching the way beer fizzed in his glass. This account is even given by historian Howard Peckham in his book *The Making of the University of Michigan*.

Donald Glaser with his bubble chamber, which won him the 1960 Nobel Prize in physics. *Lawrence Berkeley National Laboratory.*

Throughout his life, however, Glaser adamantly denied that there was any truth to this story about a eureka moment over a beer at the Pretzel Bell, calling it "totally wrong" and "perverted by journalists." He set the record straight about beer's role in his invention in an oral history interview for the Lawrence Berkeley National Laboratory, where he went to work on larger and more sophisticated bubble chambers in 1959.

Prior to Glaser's invention, physicists mainly used gas chambers to trace the paths of subatomic particles generated in atom smashers. The particles would pass through a gas cloud, leaving behind a trail that could be photographed and studied. The bubble chamber replaced the gas with superheated liquid, which could potentially show the particles' paths in much greater detail. The trouble was figuring out what liquid should be used.

Glaser first experimented with a compound known as diethyl ether before having his true eureka moment. What about beer? "Why fool around with all these exotics?" he remembered thinking. "Water is probably out of the question, but I decided 'What the hell?'"

He didn't get the results he wanted. Heating the beer caused it to spew all over the lab, making the entire physics building reek of rancid brew. Unfortunately for Glaser, alcohol was not allowed on campus. That wasn't the only problem. "The other problem was that the chairman was a very devout teetotaler, and he was furious," Glaser recalled. "He almost fired me on the spot."

Donald Glaser's invention, which led to the discovery of even smaller particles called quarks, won him the Nobel Prize in 1960. In his acceptance speech, he said that his work in nuclear physics was "especially remote from the experience of ordinary daily life," apparently forgetting that nothing could be more a part of ordinary daily life than beer.

As for the Pretzel Bell, a portrait of Glaser hung on a wall otherwise full of pictures of athletes right up until the bar sadly closed in 1985.

———•———

Students for a Democratic Society. The White Panther Party. Vietnam War protests. Student sit-ins. Marijuana activists. Police riots.

Ann Arbor in the late 1960s and early 1970s is the stuff of baby boomer legend, and it is best left to members of that generation to continue mythologizing their youth for the everlasting benefit of all mankind. But whatever else might be said of the era, there's no denying some really good music came out of it. And although the focus may have mostly been on different sorts of mind-altering chemicals, beer was still right there on the scene alongside all those long-haired hippie freaks and rock-and-roll misfits.

In fact, at least one well-known Ann Arbor band from that time owes its very existence to beer. In a May 31, 1974 *Ann Arbor Sun* interview, George Frayne IV explained how he and guitarist John Tichy formed country rock band Commander Cody and His Lost Planet Airmen in 1967: "We started...as a last ditch effort by which me and Tichy could get some more bread so we could drink some more beer." You know Commander Cody if you've ever grooved to rockabilly classics like "Lost in the Ozone" and "Hot Rod Lincoln."

The same year Commander Cody first gathered his Airmen, some guy named Jim Morrison and his band, the Doors, came to Ann Arbor to play a homecoming gig at the prestigious University of Michigan Intramural Sports Building. The show turned into a disaster when the Doors took the stage minus their frontman, who, according to a 2010 *Michigan Today* interview with late keyboardist Ray Manzarek, was "drunk as a skunk." When Morrison finally came out, he didn't sing but instead staggered around insulting and swearing at his shocked audience of mostly clean-cut football players and their elegantly dressed girlfriends.

But one face in the crowd that evening, University of Michigan dropout Jim Osterberg, was actually inspired by Morrison's drunken performance, noted Ann Arbor historian Alan Glenn. Not long after, Osterberg joined a band called the Stooges and adopted his own in-your-face stage persona, Iggy Pop.

Like Morrison before him, Iggy's wild onstage antics also often antagonized audiences, memorably resulting in the 1976 live album, *Metallic K.O.*, described by renowned rock critic Lester Bangs as "the only rock album I know where you can actually hear hurled beer bottles breaking against guitar strings." More recently, thesmokinggun.com published Iggy and the Stooges' 2012 tour rider—the document the band gives to concert venues outlining what they need for their performance. Among the twenty-eight-page rider's humorous, typo-filled list of requirements and requests is this:

> *1 case of big bottles of good, premium beer. You decide. But remember, I might ask you to taste a bottle, so buy something nice!! Here's a clue—it's probably won't start with a letter "B" and end with "udweiser." Unless it's Czech.*

Iggy Pop is not the only famous Ann Arbor musician to request beer for his performances. Just before his 1975 album *Beautiful Loser* launched his career into the stratosphere, all Bob Seger wanted from one concert promoter was a six-pack of Heineken for his tour bus. Unfortunately for Seger, there was no beer to be found at the rustic outdoor venue. It had all just been dumped into a nearby lake during a police raid.

That concert promoter, Robert Jr Whitall, remembered the event very well. "It took place on August 9, 1974, the day Richard Nixon resigned," he said. Today, Whitall runs *Big City Rhythm & Blues* magazine from Royal Oak, but he was "just a poor college kid" when he and his late friend Steve Post had the idea to throw a "big barn dance party" on the Ypsilanti Township farm where Post lived. The farm, adjoining Ford Lake, was being sold, and a party seemed like a good way to say goodbye to the property. But it was to be no ordinary party.

"I used to golf with Bob Seger's manager, Punch Andrews," recalled Whitall. "Bob agreed to come play at our barn party, and it turned out to be his last gig before he hit the big time."

Original poster for the "Barn Dance" concert at a farm on Textile Road. *Mike Gould and Robert Jr Whitall.*

Whitall and Post lined up three other bands—the Rabbits, the Martian Entropy Band and the Rockets—and printed up flyers to distribute around Ann Arbor and Ypsilanti advertising their "Barn Dance for All the Animals." "Five dollars a head, all the beer you could drink, and Bob Seger: what's not to like?" Mike Gould of the Martian Entropy Band remembered in a 2007 *Ann Arbor Observer* article.

The barn, being a barn, had no power, so Whitall's crew ran a cable out to illegally tap an electrical box on the side of Textile Road. They bought forty kegs of beer—Whitall believes it was Molson Canadian—and forty cases of wine and set it all up in a picnic area on top of a hill. Whitall's fiancée collected the five-dollar "donations" from cars as they drove up the dirt road, though as Whitall recalled, most of the "immense crowd" parked across a field and just walked in for free.

The first two bands went on, then Seger took the stage and everything seemed to be going well, at least until Whitall looked out the window of the farmhouse where he was sitting and saw cops coming up the road. Someone had reported the party to the state police and the Liquor Control Commission to boot.

"We didn't have a liquor license, but that's why we asked for donations," recalled Whitall. "We weren't selling beer, and our lawyer had said that would be fine." The cops would have none of it, so Whitall made a decision. "I sent a runner up the hill and told him to throw the kegs in the lake," he said. "If we couldn't have them, the cops weren't going to get them either."

Gould remembered being in the barn loft helping put on the light show behind Seger when he looked out and saw people rolling kegs of beer down the hill and into Ford Lake with a splash. Steve Post and Whitall's lawyer were hauled off by the cops, but the party continued, beer-free.

Shortly after, Seger's set was over, and he asked for his Heineken. "I had to scramble to find someone who could go get him the beer so we could satisfy his rider," remembered Whitall. "But he stuck around for the Rockets, and it was great seeing him dancing in the barn—it was such a low-key and wonderful event."

Local legend has long held that the kegs of beer are still lying somewhere at the bottom of the lake, but Whitall said that the police came back later with a dive team to retrieve them. And a court eventually ruled that the cops had no right to bust the barn dance in the first place, but as Whitall wryly noted, "That ruling didn't do us any good 10 years later."

CHAPTER 10

BUBBLING UNDER

I f there's any era in America's beer history potentially more depressing than the prohibition years, it's the period between the end of World War II and the latter half of the 1980s. All throughout those decades, increasing industrialization along with mergers and consolidations combined to gradually reduce the number of breweries in the country from about five hundred to fewer than one hundred, with most of those being large mass producers of swill.

To be sure, many other factors contributed to this sad state of affairs. Beer drinkers were not only becoming increasingly brand-conscious—in part due to the rise of television advertising—but TV also nudged the once diverse regional markets for beer into becoming as homogenized as American-brewed beer itself.

Historians offer several theories for why postwar Americans began overwhelmingly preferring light-bodied, relatively bland beer that we need not delve into here. Suffice it to say—and as blessedly hard as it may be for today's under-thirty beer lovers to imagine—for many long years, almost all commercial brew in the United States was indeed like making love in a canoe.

Also now hard to imagine: Ann Arbor, with its reputation for hippies, drugs and left-wing radicalism, was prior to the 1960s a conservative town of generally Republican-leaning politics and "dry" sentiment. In a reminiscence published in the spring 2003 *Michigan Quarterly Review*, alumna Anne Stevenson ('54) remembered the 10:30 p.m. weekday student curfew (at least for young ladies). She recounted a time she and her dorm-mate were

Until 1960, Ann Arborites had to congregate in private clubs like the Moose Lodge if they wanted booze with their beer. *From a June 1956 edition of the* Ann Arbor News. *All rights reserved. Reprinted with permission.*

caught and almost expelled for trying to sneak two male friends into their room for beers. And far from offering romantic Parisian-style cafés in which to discuss James Joyce, Gertrude Stein, Virginia Woolf and Ezra Pound over drinks, the Ann Arbor of Stevenson's memory had just two restaurants, Metzger's and the Pretzel Bell, "where you could drink wine or beer, and then only if you were over twenty-one and produced your ID card."

In fact, in Stevenson's day, wine and beer were the only alcoholic options available in any bar or restaurant. A city ordinance of the time allowed only private clubs, like the Moose Lodge or the hoity-toity Town Club, to sell liquor by the glass. And, of course, the dry line along Division Street was still in place, keeping Michigan students, and anyone else living on that side of town, sober and virtuous.

As the countercultural movement spilled beyond the confines of Beat poetry readings in smoky coffee shops and out into the street to blossom in its disaffected zenith, public attitudes toward drinking (and many other things) began to gradually but dramatically change. Liquor by the glass for bars and restaurants was legalized in 1960, and new establishments began to spring up around town. A guy named Dominick DeVarti bought an old house on Monroe Street across from the University of Michigan Law Quad and started what would become Ann Arbor's most popular beer garden. Red Fraser purchased a failed business out on Packard Street and turned it into townie favorite Fraser's Pub, which celebrated its fiftieth anniversary in 2012. The Old Heidelberg on North Main Street, going strong to this day, joined the Old German and Metzger's restaurants in keeping Tree Town's German beer and food traditions alive.

Metzger's, in its original Washington Street location, was even where the modern environmentalist movement was launched over pitchers of beer in 1969. Historian James Tobin tells of how University of Michigan zoology and botany students met for drinks at Metzger's after long days spent in the lab. Their informal beer and bull sessions soon turned into planning

Walter Metzger (left) takes ownership of Metzger's Restaurant from father Bill Metzger (center-left). *From a June 1959 edition of the* Ann Arbor News. *All rights reserved. Reprinted with permission.*

meetings for a multiday "Teach-In on the Environment," leading up to the first Earth Day on April 22, 1970.

Also by the end of the 1960s, the century-old Division Street dry line was finally abolished by an overwhelming vote of Ann Arborites. No longer would students (or faculty) have to walk all the way to the Pretzel Bell or Metzger's to enjoy a glass or four of draft beer. Of course, many of the day's rebellious youngsters were more interested in marijuana and other illicit narcotics. The March 3, 1969 *Ann Arbor News* quoted an unnamed detective on the city's suddenly brisk drug trade: "[I]n 1967 we had a drug arrest total of over 50 persons. Last year that figure was 115. It's still climbing."

But beer would make a comeback with the underage set just a few years later. Pioneer High student David Feldt said in the December 9, 1973 *Ann Arbor News* that his friends drank more "with beer readily accessible to most students—no matter what their age." A tenth-grade

The recently restored Beer Depot sign, shown here in 1967, is a downtown Ann Arbor landmark. *Ann Arbor District Library.*

girl agreed, noting that among her circle fewer "are taking pills but more are drinking beer." Huron High senior Andrew Byrnes added that most parents knew that their kids drank or smoked pot, but the majority "feel drinking is socially acceptable."

Actually, for a time in the 1970s, Michigan's legal drinking age was eighteen. Some Ann Arborites fondly remember high school days cruising through the drive-throughs of places like the Beer Depot or the Beer Vault, both of which continued to operate thanks to a grandfather clause in the state's law against drive-through alcohol sales.

"The Vault was owned by a friendly Korean guy," recalled longtime townie Jim Rees. "The service was great: You'd drive in, and he'd pull the empties out of the trunk and put in full cases."

But going out for a beer in downtown Ann Arbor in the 1960s and '70s was a much different proposition than it is in today's gentrified bars and upscale restaurants. Some areas could be rough. Mark Hodesh, who owned the Fleetwood Diner in the early 1970s, had a front-row seat for the beer-fueled brawls between townies and students that took place regularly across the street at the Schwaben Inn. All Music Guide founder Michael Erlewine remembered one huge fight at the Schwaben—so called due to its location

The former Schwaben Halle on Ashley Street, now a furniture store and office space. *Photo by Nicole Rupersburg.*

in the "Schwaben Halle" built by Ann Arbor's longest-lasting German society—that required nine police cars to break up.

Other areas, like the infamous East Ann Street block of dives and pool halls that inspired Bob Seger's hit "Mainstreet," could be downright dangerous. According to retired police sergeant Michael Logghe, one bar, the Derby, "was the site of many fights, stabbings, and shootings," including two murders in 1974.

By the early 1980s, most of the rough-and-tumble dives and blue-collar beer halls of Ann Arbor had given way to shops, offices and drinking establishments better suited to the yuppified tastes (and larger wallets) of the professional and collegiate types that had been slowly taking over the old working-class black and German neighborhoods. Signs soon appeared that Ann Arborites—if not Americans generally—were at last ready to expand their beer horizons beyond Miller Lite and Pabst Blue Ribbon.

———

Serial restaurateur Andy Gulvezan opened Ann Arbor's first modern beer bar, the Full Moon Café, on Main Street in March 1982. Known for his creative concepts, Gulvezan was described as a "mustachioed, swaggering personality" in the May 1982 *Ann Arbor Observer* review of his new venture. The bar was unlike others of the time, evoking a turn-of-the-century vibe thanks to such décor as the Victorian back bar from a pre-prohibition Upper Peninsula saloon and several ornate cast-iron globe lamps.

But the Full Moon's most unusual feature was its huge beer selection, which boasted hundreds of different bottled varieties, mostly "exotic" imports like Pilsner Urquell, Foster's, Grolsch, Bitburger and Bass Ale but also including some from the closer-to-home Frankenmuth Brewery. John Pruder remembered (barely) the "Full Moon Beer Tour," where drinking numerous different brews would get the triumphant barfly a reward, like a Full Moon T-shirt or, as Pruder and his friends liked to joke, "a free liver transplant."

Gulvezan later bought the Flame, a decades-old gay bar on West Washington Street, and contracted with the Joseph Huber Brewing Company to supply Harry's Lager and Harry's Light, named after longtime bartender Harry Tselios. They were the only beers served there, and patrons described them in glowing terms like "Disgusting!" and "It sucks!"

Longtime Flame bartender Harry Tselios and the beers named after him. *Peter Yates, for the April 1989 edition of the* Ann Arbor Observer.

Less than a year after the Full Moon opened, "cheerful, clean-cut collegiate types" Gary Treer, Roy More and Jeff More opened a new restaurant, hoping to offer State Street diners "something in the mid-price range that isn't Italian," as they said in the April 1983 *Ann Arbor Observer*. The partners wanted a snappy, one-word name to capture the elegant dining experience they hoped to provide their customers and, after a long process, settled on using Roy's middle name for the place. Ashley's, Ann Arbor's most famous and enduring beer bar, was born.

"It was a totally different place at the time," remembered Marc Grasso, who started as a busboy soon after Ashley's opened and later became a bartender. "It had carpeting, it had a salad bar, it had a couple domestic beer taps. We wore vests and bowties to bus." The partners quickly gave up their upscale concept, he said, when they realized that they could better capitalize on something no other State Street restaurant of the time had: a liquor license.

"They added this big porcelain Warsteiner fountain tap—there are still holes in the bar where it was—and that was something nobody had ever seen," Grasso recalled. Within a few years, Treer left, the carpet was stripped to expose the wood floors, the salad bar was removed, several more taps

"Cheerful, clean-cut collegiate types" Gary Treer, Jeff More and Roy More pose in front of what would become Michigan's most prominent beer bar. *Peter Yates, for the April 1983 edition of the* Ann Arbor Observer.

were installed and the word "Pub" was officially added to the sign. The cooler filled up with bottled imports and obscure-for-the-time beers. And, said Grasso, Jeff More openly adopted a new business philosophy: "We need to educate the customers."

"I thought that idea was ridiculous," Grasso remembered. "'We just need to give people whatever beer they want,' was my attitude as a bartender. Well, as we now know, Jeff was right. There are plenty of beers people want; they just might not know about them."

Another bar, whose legend was already well established by this time, also embraced "alternative" beers, along with an alternative way of doing business. Founded in 1969, Ann Arbor's original bohemian bar, the Del Rio on West Washington Street, was an "attempt to devise and create a democratic workplace in a local barroom," in the words of its co-owner Ernie Harburg. All employees—cooks, bartenders and waitstaff—met monthly to collectively decide how to run the bar, and they did so for thirty-five years. Everything from hiring and firing decisions to menu choices to, yes, the beer selection was subject to consensus from the group. Notes from one of these employee meetings suggests a lively discussion over whether to serve more "imported bottled beer," with the con side arguing against nonrecyclable

Bartender Marc Grasso at the legendary Del Rio bar, circa 1992. *Peter Yates, for the* Ann Arbor Observer.

import bottles and in favor of keeping money in the local economy and the pro side saying of the beer, "it's better."

What was ultimately decided about the imported beer is not recorded. But according to Grasso, who also bartended there, the Del was the first bar in Ann Arbor to sell beer from a certain Kalamazoo brewery founded in 1985. And that wasn't even the Del's first foray into Michigan-brewed beer. Several years before that, the hippie bar also stocked bottles from the first microbrewery to open east of Colorado: Chelsea's Real Ale Company.

———

"Oh, we sold a lot of beer at the Del Rio," remembered Ted Badgerow. "I showed up with some cases, said, 'Here, try this!' and people really liked it."

Badgerow was only a few years removed from his first contact with "real beer," as he calls it. During his annual bike tour around Michigan in 1978, he stopped in at a friend's house near Grand Rapids. "You look hot," his friend said, and poured him a cold brew. "I said, 'Man, this is really good. Is it German?'" he recalled. "He told me, 'No, I brewed it.' I didn't believe him."

From that point on, Badgerow was hooked. He immediately began homebrewing himself, receiving favorable comments from everyone he shared his beers with. Several people even suggested that he start his own brewery. He didn't take such talk seriously, at least not at first. The "Aha!" moment came next summer, when he was helping out on a dairy farm owned by another friend, Gordon Averill.

"Gordon was going through rough times; in fact, all the small dairy farms were going broke," Badgerow said. "We were looking into this beautiful stainless steel tank full of milk lamenting how little money it would bring when I said, 'How much could we make if we filled it with beer?'" Now Averill was hooked. The two partners opened the Real Ale Company three years later.

It was not an easy process. Badgerow and Averill had to raise capital in the midst of a deep recession. They had to deal with clueless state bureaucrats who had never even heard of anyone trying to open a brewery before. And they had to find a location that had a desirable combination of good water, adequate brewing space and potential customers.

But with $12,000 from ten investors, some repurposed farm equipment, a makeshift bottling line and plenty of old-fashioned elbow grease, the first new commercial brewery in Michigan in three decades whirred to life in September 1982 on the second floor of the clock tower building in downtown Chelsea. Badgerow served as president, CEO and head brewer, while Averill handled all physical plant aspects of the operation.

Badgerow's process was straightforward: "I just crank up the stereo, stoke up the boiler and brew some ale," he told *Time* magazine for a July 25, 1983 article on this curious new microbrewery thing. He brewed in three-and-a-half-barrel batches, usually beginning at two or three o'clock in the morning and finishing up around six or seven o'clock. Then, all of it was hand-bottled and labeled four at a time. There were three styles: a porter, a stout and one they simply called Chelsea Ale, an English-style bitter.

For the most part, Badgerow and Averill distributed their product themselves (this was allowed in Michigan at the time) in four-packs and cases of twenty-four, running routes from Detroit to Grand Rapids and up to Traverse City. Because the beer was unfiltered and bottled with live yeast ("That's the definition of real ale," Badgerow said), they took pains to emphasize to each of their accounts the importance of properly refrigerating the beer so it didn't go bad. They never attempted to distribute in draft for a variety of reasons, including space and equipment limitations as well as lower potential profit margins.

"The Sidetrack bar in Ypsilanti was our biggest outlet, with the former Big Ten Party Store in Ann Arbor our second biggest," Badgerow recalled. "We sold everything we could brew."

Word spread fast. A reporter from the Chelsea newspaper visited the brewery. Then one from the *Ann Arbor News*. Then came television crews from Detroit. Then the team from *Time*.

"Except for a few radio ads in Ann Arbor, we didn't advertise," said Badgerow. "Some people thought we were nuts, but we felt our product spoke for itself. We sold t-shirts and hats. We ended up on the cover of *Brewers Digest*. Because we were such a new, unique thing at the time, we didn't lack for publicity."

Indeed not. At one point, the Hall & Oates tour bus even pulled up on its way to Canada. "They were driving through town for whatever reason, stopped at the brewery, and some roadies came up and bought sixty or seventy cases of beer," said Badgerow, who performs as a musician himself. "We gave some fun tours and parties. We were a rock-and-roll brewery."

But the good times wouldn't last long. The manual labor required to do everything was inefficient and costly, especially for an admitted mom and pop operation, as was sourcing most of the malt and hops from England.

Chelsea's Real Ale Company, which lasted barely more than a year, was the first microbrewery east of Colorado. *Collection of Ted Badgerow. Photo by David Bardallis.*

This made for bad economics: cases of Real Ale beer sold for $20.00, the most expensive on the market, but cost $25.60 to produce. "The more we brewed, the more we lost," said Badgerow.

Inadequate sanitation procedures and quality control issues didn't help the brewery's reputation either. Several longtime Ann Arbor homebrewers and beer drinkers remember getting bottles that had sour or other off flavors or were "gushers."

With no financial backing to see it through the rough patch, the Real Ale Company closed at the end of 1983 when the lease on the clock tower space was not renewed. Badgerow then occasionally lectured on brewing and beer styles at the University of Michigan before opening a homebrew supply store on Ann Street in the mid-1980s. He was instrumental in the founding of the Ann Arbor Brewers Guild homebrew club (about which more later) and remains an avid homebrewer to this day. Plus, he said, he hasn't ruled out a return to the commercial brewing business, occasionally scouting locations around the Ypsilanti area where he lives.

A young Larry Bell sampling the wares. *Bell's Brewery.*

Every end contains within it the seeds of a new beginning, as the old saying goes. One Monday morning, a twenty-four-year-old sporting a beard and a backpack popped into the Real Ale Company and woke Ted Badgerow where he slept on the floor. They sat on an old sofa together and smoked while the young man asked questions about beer and brewing for a few hours before leaving to hitchhike his way back to Kalamazoo. Three years later, Larry Bell took what he learned from Badgerow (as well as some equipment he bought from the failed Real Ale Company) and founded the brewery that today bears his name.

"I was homebrewing a lot, watching what they were doing, buying beer from them, definitely interested in what they had going on," remembered Bell. At the time, he was living at a group house on Washtenaw Avenue while he worked at various Ann Arbor restaurants and waited to start a job at a friend's new jazz club, the Bird of Paradise, that was supposed to open soon.

"I didn't have a car back then, but I sometimes borrowed my girlfriend's to drive down to the Fink Brothers homebrew supply store in Dundee," remembered Bell. "The Bird of Paradise ended up not opening until a few years later, and I had better opportunities in Kalamazoo, so I moved back."

By the time he started the then Kalamazoo Brewing Company, Bell had acquired Badgerow's thirty-gallon soup kettle. "I gave Ted $100 for it," he said. "We used it only as a mash tun in our three-vessel, one-barrel system because there were no controls on it."

Bell's has, of course, grown a wee bit from its initial production of 135 barrels. It's now the seventh-largest craft brewery (fourteenth largest overall) by sales volume in the country, producing more than 200,000 barrels annually and distributing such wildly popular beers as Oberon and Two-Hearted ales in eighteen states, Puerto Rico and Washington, D.C.

Homebrewing was not exactly legal when Jeff Renner started doing it as a graduate student at Michigan in 1973. "It was not only not legal, people hardly knew what to make of it," he said. He had recently acquired a taste for beers beyond "the yellow fizzy stuff" during a Fourth of July weekend trip to an island on the Canadian side of Lake Huron.

"My friend brought a case of Molson Stock Ale with him," Renner recalled. "It was an amber beer that tasted hoppier and maltier, just completely different from anything I had ever had before."

Jeff Renner in 1983, using another sort of yeast to make breads he still sells around town. *Peter Yates, for the* Ann Arbor Observer.

There weren't too many imports in those days to satisfy his new yearnings for flavor, so Renner's do-it-yourself inclinations naturally led him to brew his own. Like Larry Bell, he made trips down to the Fink Brothers store in Dundee to pick up how-to books, equipment, malt extract, pelletized hops and other ingredients. "They were one of the first homebrew stores around," he said. In Ann Arbor, the former Big Ten Party Store and Hertler Brothers (now Downtown Home and Garden) also sold beermaking supplies.

A teacher and a baker, Renner mostly brewed by himself until the early 1980s, when he saw a flyer posted at Big Ten advertising a meeting of other homebrewers. It sounded like a good idea.

"We met at the Burns Park home of a botany professor, who actually was teaching homebrewing as part of his classes at Michigan," Renner recalled. "There were about eight or ten of us, and we just stood around and shared beers."

But the seeds of the Ann Arbor Brewers Guild were not officially sown until a few years later. In 1986, Renner got together with several other homebrewers, including Rolf Wucherer and Ted Badgerow, whose Fermentations homebrew store was open for business on Ann Street. As Badgerow remembered it, they met in the basement of the Old Heidelberg over several glasses of Dortmunder Dark and came up with a name.

Ann Arbor has been a hotbed of homebrewing for decades. *From the September 16, 1992 edition of the* Ann Arbor News. *All rights reserved. Reprinted with permission.*

"There were some silly suggestions, but I argued for 'Ann Arbor Brewers Guild' because I thought that was classy, and I liked evoking the old idea of trade guilds," said Renner.

Meetings took place at members' homes (a practice that continues today) and for years consisted of only about "half a dozen to ten" people sharing beer samples, talking about recipes and learning from one another. By the early 1990s, however, the growing popularity of the hobby had brought in so many new enthusiasts that the meetings began to get somewhat unwieldy. "We had become a club that definitely could no longer just sit around the table," said Renner.

And with so many people now enjoying good, flavorful beer of their own creation, it was just a matter of time before conditions became right for them to begin enjoying good, flavorful beer from new commercial microbrewers.

CHAPTER 11

REBIRTH OF THE BREWS

On a cold, snowy evening in February 1995, Matt and Rene Greff sat in the window seat of Metzger's sipping their Hacker-Pschorr beers. The twenty-seven-year-old married couple often looked dreamily into each other's eyes, but on this particular occasion, their longing gazes were directed out the window and across the street at a silent and dark restaurant. The old building proclaimed the name of the now-bankrupt eatery within: Washington Street Station. Finally the couple had found the space where they would toss aside a life of soulless corporate jobs and follow their dream of opening a brewery.

Several years before that night, Barry Seifer longed for the hoppy microbrewed pale ales he used to drink before moving from his native Berkeley, California, to Ann Arbor in the late 1980s. Not only did his new hometown not have a microbrewery, the law also made it impossible for such establishments to exist. More than thirty states allowed brew-on-premise restaurants—commonly called brewpubs—but Michigan was not one of them.

At least not yet. Before long, Seifer found himself lobbying the state legislature on behalf of a proposed brewpub and microbrewery law. The effort met with success—albeit not without compromises—in late 1992, and Seifer had the go-ahead for his own venture: Grizzly Peak Brewing Company, which he named after Berkeley's scenic Grizzly Peak Boulevard.

By 1995, it was a race to see which Washington Street brewpub would open first, Arbor or Grizzly Peak. Excitement built among the members of the Ann Arbor Brewers Guild, along with the rest of the town's beer-loving faithful. In all of Michigan, there were only a handful of other brewpubs, and Tree Town was about to get two more, just to itself. (For context, the July 1995 issue of Detroit's late, lamented *Orbit* magazine advertised the "largest beer-tasting in Michigan history" with 150 beers, only about 7 of which were brewed in the state.)

"There was definitely a bit of a rivalry to see who could get open first," said Jon Carlson, who replaced Barry Seifer as Grizzly Peak partner when Seifer withdrew. The new partnership had changed plans to open in what is now Café Zola when they instead purchased the space occupied by the Old German restaurant from the retiring Bud Metzger.

For the Greffs, it was a simple matter of survival. After months of work gutting, refinishing and equipping the former Washington Street Station, "we were up to our eyeballs in debt and bills—we had to get open and start generating revenue," said Matt.

On July 12, 1995, the much-anticipated Arbor Brewing threw open its doors for what was to be an invitation-only soft opening. Unfortunately for the Greffs, a friend had sent out the invitation via "the Internet of the time: email," and a line of people that stretched down the block and around the corner greeted Matt and Rene for their 7:00 p.m. opening. The next six hours were a complete disaster.

"Matt wanted to brew; that's all we knew," recalled Rene. "We had no experience running a restaurant and no idea what we were doing. We couldn't get food to tables. It was a nightmare."

It went so horribly, she said, they closed for a week to regroup before opening again—during the week of the Ann Arbor Art Fairs, the busiest time of the year. "It was a week of the exact same nightmare," said Matt. "Only worse," added Rene.

The next several months turned out to be rough for the Greffs. Matt remembered one bad night where he had to inform a table that their entrées just weren't coming. "The guy picked up his soft pretzel, threw it at my chest and told me, 'You should be ashamed of yourself,'" he said. By 1996, the two were ready to throw in the towel and declare bankruptcy until their lawyer informed them they would be indentured servants for the rest of their lives, trying to pay off their investors. They had no choice but to make the business work.

Arbor's beer, brewed on the same seven-barrel system in use today, did sell well. Offerings began with brews based on recipes from Matt's homebrewing repertoire, like Big Ben House Mild, Red Snapper Amber Ale (since reclassified as a "roasted pale ale") and Faricy Fest Irish Stout. Gradually,

Matt and Rene Greff in 1995. *J. Adrian Wylie, for the* Ann Arbor Observer.

other beers were added, such as Bavarian Bliss Hefeweizen, Olde No. 22 German Alt and Sacred Cow IPA, which was named by a skeptical former bar manager. "Fairly early on, I made a small, two-barrel batch of IPA to put on the hand pull," said Matt. "I just wanted a beer for me, something big and hoppy to drink after a long day. I told our bar manager I wasn't changing it even if customers thought it was too bitter or foamy or warm or whatever. 'Oh,' he said, 'So it's your sacred cow!'" But Matt was wrong: The IPA sold quickly, as did the next, larger batch. Today, it remains the pub's top-selling beer.

When it opened about a month after Arbor, Grizzly Peak's start, while not without hiccups, went more smoothly. But one needed change became apparent early on: the brewpub couldn't keep selling its English-style ales in traditional British half-yard glasses. "They kept breaking and were so hard to keep in stock," remembered Carlson. "But we didn't want to switch to plastic half-yards because you can't drink good beer out of plastic."

One of the first brewers at Grizzly Peak was Ron Jeffries, who so impressed Carlson and his partners that they gave him a corporate brewer role, which soon blossomed into a highly significant relationship for craft beer lovers in Ann Arbor and beyond. "Within a month, we realized how awesome Ron was," said Carlson. "He went on to help us open every other brewpub we've done, from North Peak in Traverse City to Bastone in Royal Oak to Blue Tractor here."

By 1997, following a shakeup in the way they managed the business, the Greffs were finally beginning to feel that they hadn't made a big mistake opening Arbor. Their own beer was selling, and they even started something new to help foster further beer exploration and appreciation among Ann Arborites: monthly style tasting events. Just the second tasting ever held cemented what would become a signature series for the brewpub.

"We didn't plan to do them monthly at first, but when we did a Michigan-only tasting in June or July and it was wildly successful, that's when we said, 'OK, we're on to something," said Rene.

"In our own little world, we take credit for starting the whole Michigan Summer Beer Festival tradition," Matt laughed. "I mean, not really, but Rex Halfpenny of *Michigan Beer Guide* did point out at the time that nobody had ever brought Michigan breweries all together to showcase their wares like that."

Nor did they plan for the tastings—now in their sixteenth year—to last so long either. "We keep waiting for them to run their course," said Rene. "But month after month, year after year, they continue to sell out."

—•—

Although circumstances had forced him to pull out of the Grizzly Peak partnership, Barry Seifer never forgot his dream of creating hoppy West Coast ales in Ann Arbor. About the time the Greffs were finding their footing, he was back with a new business plan that combined his beery aspirations with another yeastful endeavor: breadmaking.

"Brewing and baking are both management of fermentation," said Seifer. "It just made sense to do both." The result was Brewbakers Craft Brewery and Bakehouse, a conscious effort to revive "the tradition of the small-scale, pre-Prohibition local brewery," as the labels on the bottles would later read. It opened in July 1997 in the basement of 410 North Fourth Avenue in Kerrytown, where Seifer and his partner and now wife, Sarah Minor, installed a fifteen-barrel brew system and a custom-built round brick oven to make the kinds of artisanal, French-style breads he went to Montreal for a year to learn about. The location was less than ideal, but because the new venture was licensed to distribute as a microbrewery, the city required it to be within a manufacturing zone.

Bottles from the short-lived Brewbakers brewery in Ann Arbor's Kerrytown. *Collection of Sean Bachman. Photo by David Bardallis.*

"It was a compromise of sorts. The Kerrytown location allowed for a lively retail space while, oddly enough, meeting the zoning requirements," recalled Seifer. "Our goal was to become a neighborhood destination but also a microbrewery with distribution throughout the area."

Ron Jeffries briefly joined the new brewery, but it was mainly Seifer, Michigan beer pioneer Matt Allyn and brewer Derek Foster who came up with the general run of Brewbakers beers, which included London Porter, Chestnut Ale (an English-style bitter), Scotch Ale, German Style Helles, Raspberry Ale and Pacific Coast Pale Ale, which to Seifer's delight immediately won an award. "The first batch of pale ale that we brewed was entered into a competition of Michigan microbrews, and it took the top spot in its category as well as best in show. It was a really lovely thing," he said.

Karl Dickinson, a fellow onetime Californian who worked as a baker, remembered his first encounter with both Seifer and the Pacific Coast Pale Ale. "He took me back into the brewery and poured me a pale ale straight out of the tank. I don't think the bottling line had even arrived yet," he said. "I immediately fell in love with the beer and with the ambiance of the place, which was all cobblestone and marble—really old-fashioned."

Customers could buy beer by the bottle and drink it on the premises, which included an outdoor patio, and watch the brewing and breadmaking processes. In fact, they could do more than watch, if they wanted. "We had the space divided in half, with the brewery behind glass and the bakery open," recalled Seifer. "We understood how powerful it is to be the village bakery. People would ask if they could come in to work, and we'd let them cut the dough and shape the loaves while we talked politics, art, children—everything. We still have friendships with some of the people who came in to help. The Europeans especially got what we were doing."

Brewbakers beers were distributed in bottles and kegs to bars and stores in Ann Arbor. The short-lived Jimmy's Double-A Bar and Grill on Main Street even served Pacific Coast Pale Ale (and later brews like the Russian Imperial Stout) in casks. One of the largest accounts was the Ann Arbor Whole Foods Market. "The fellow who ran their beer department adored our beers and was a big promoter of them," recalled Seifer. "It was all we could do to keep him supplied."

Word got out beyond Ann Arbor as well. The executive chef at the Ritz Carlton's restaurant in Dearborn used Brewbakers table bread exclusively and also carried its beer. Dickinson remembered supplying some big parties at the luxury hotel. "When Daimler bought Chrysler, and the executives hosted a multimillion-dollar event, we made all the bread for that," he said. "We made a four-foot pretzel, a baguette you could see from the back of a warehouse, all kinds of things."

It seemed Brewbakers was on the verge of becoming something big when the end came in the spring of 1999. Dickinson remembered how abrupt it was. "Everything was going great, we were making the bread same as the day before, when Barry and Sarah came in and told us to shut down the mixer. His face was white as a sheet when he said Brewbakers was closing and not opening back up," he said. "It happened that quickly."

The company's lead investor had sold his business and was liquidating all his local investments, including in Brewbakers, and moving out of town. "When he pulled out, so did everyone else," said Seifer. "We decided we had to fold it up."

Today, Dickinson works at Arbor Brewing and hopes to soon get back into his true passion, making bread. Seifer runs a successful biotech startup from an office at—in another of those cosmic coincidences—the old Tech Brewery building on Jones Drive. He doesn't homebrew and has no desire to open another brewery.

"It's great that beer has taken off in Michigan like it has," he said. "I'm just pleased to have been a tiny part of that." And although he's not making it himself, Seifer's dream of fresh, hoppy beer is realized whenever he goes into Arbor Brewing and orders a Sacred Cow IPA from the hand pull. That makes him "really, really happy."

———

Even as one Ann Arbor brewery closed, another that had been in the planning stages since 1995 was getting ready to open. In 1999, siblings Todd and Scott Leopold founded Leopold Brothers of Ann Arbor in a renovated garage on Main Street a few blocks south of downtown. Their goal was to make it "the world's first environmentally sustainable brewery."

But why do it in Ann Arbor and not in their native Colorado, epicenter of the 1990s microbrewing revolution? "The Denver-Boulder area was already home to fourteen breweries when we were putting together our plan, and we thought that market was saturated," said Todd. "Of

Brewer Todd Leopold and environmental engineer Scott Leopold prepare to open Leopold Bros. of Ann Arbor in 1999. *J. Adrian Wylie, for the* Ann Arbor Observer.

course, more than fourteen new breweries opened here in 2012 alone, so obviously we were wrong!"

Scott, with a master's degree in environmental engineering from Stanford, designed the brewhouse, and Todd, who had trained at the Doemens school in Munich, served as brewer. That German education showed itself not just in beers like the top-selling Red Lager, brewed with Munich malt and Hallertau hops, but in the layout of the taproom, which was spacious and open, featuring long beerhall-style table seating. A large repository of board games and an eclectic jukebox, curated by Todd, contributed to the casual, communal atmosphere that appealed to the hipster crowd, which migrated in large numbers when the Del Rio, also known for a vast and quirky music collection, closed at the end of 2003. (Noise complaints had by then unfortunately put an end to the brewery's regular live music sessions.)

As a microbrewery, Leopold Brothers was licensed to distribute its beers, and Todd initially bottled a number of them; the Red Lager was joined by a Golden Lager, Pilsner, Hefeweizen, Schwarzbier, Oktoberfest, Porter and Pale Ale. But his focus soon changed. "We distributed bottled beer for only a matter of months," Todd recalled. "When the price for a distilling license dropped from $10,000 to $500, we sold our beer filler and bought a still."

Bottled selections from Leopold Bros. of Ann Arbor. *Collection of Sean Bachman. Photo by David Bardallis.*

Soon, Leopold Brothers was producing vodka, gin, absinthe and specialty liqueurs, some of which were distributed outside the taproom. "By 2001, we knew as a bar we had to offer our customers something more than just beer," said Todd. (Establishments licensed as microbreweries are allowed to sell only products they make.)

The small-batch spirits gained widespread acclaim, but as Todd turned his attention to distilling more and more, many customers noticed that the quality of the beer suffered, although the taproom's status as a popular hangout never seemed to diminish.

In 2008, the old garage the brothers had renovated to house their brewery and taproom was sold, and the transaction resulted in a tax reassessment that led to sharply increased rent. Since their business had evolved in a different way than they originally anticipated, Todd and Scott chose to close the brewery and move back to Colorado, which is more friendly to small distillers. There they continue to produce small batches of their award-winning spirits, although they gave up the brewing part of their operation.

"We stopped brewing because there are so many fine breweries here in Denver, we thought it wise to focus on just one thing," said Todd.

He's not sure when Leopold Brothers liquors will be available again in Michigan, but Todd looks back on his and Scott's time in Ann Arbor warmly, especially recalling the thirsty crowds that descended on the taproom on football Saturdays, which he found to be "both thrilling and exhausting."

"Michigan has some of the best people in the world," he said.

Jon Carlson thinks back to when he first tasted beer from his former employee's new brewery. Founded by Ron Jeffries in nearby Dexter, Jolly Pumpkin Artisan Ales specializes in oak-aged sour beers, which in 2004 were not something even many experienced craft beer drinkers knew about or understood if they did.

"I thought he was nuts when I tasted it. I thought he was crazier than nuts," said Carlson. "I shared some with friends at a tailgate party, and they thought it was the worst beer they ever had. Now, of course, none of us can get enough."

Jeffries knew that his beers would be an acquired taste when he started the brewery. "Oak-aged sours are on people's radar now, but in 2004 they weren't," he said. "They were a tough sell back then." (Matt and Rene

Greff, who first brewed and bottled sour ales at Arbor in 2002 following an inspirational trip to Belgium, thought that no one but them and a few discriminating friends, including Jeffries, would drink them.)

It wasn't his original plan. At first, said Jeffries, he intended to make French- and Belgian-style witbiers and farmhouse ales along the lines of Maine's Allagash Brewing. But one evening during a backyard beer drinking session with his wife, Laurie, he asked, "Wouldn't it be nice if we could make good sour ales like this?"

"Why don't you?" she said. So he rewrote the business plan and bought some oak barrels.

According to Jeffries, they "broke all records" getting the brewery open in Dexter, going from construction to approval and brewing in under five months. The first year, the little brewery produced just 80 barrels, but then the "tough sell" quickly became easier and easier. The next year production doubled to 160 barrels, and they repeated the feat for the next several years. "We've always had trouble keeping up with the demand," said Jeffries.

Jolly Pumpkin sour ales now enjoy a growing legion of admirers, and the brewery has a national reputation, thanks in part to a 2010 *New York Times* blind tasting in which critic Eric Asimov selected Jolly Pumpkin Oro de Calabaza Golden Ale as the top Belgian-style beer.

"We were already selling as much beer as we could make, but that recognition didn't hurt," said Jeffries. "We got a lot of inquiries after that."

Jolly Pumpkin beers derive their unique taste and aroma characteristics—including what many fans lovingly call "that Jolly Pumpkin funk"—from the wild yeast and bacteria strains that live in the brewery's many oak vessels. Beers age in them anywhere from a few weeks to a few months to a year or more depending on style, and Jeffries creates blends according to the flavor profiles he desires.

"The wild organisms definitely create a distinct house characteristic," said Jeffries. "You can smell and taste it in all the beers. A lot of great sour breweries have their own signature like that."

Other popular Jolly Pumpkin beers include Bam Bière Farmhouse Ale (named by *Men's Journal* as one of the "Top 25 Beers in America"), La Roja Amber Ale and Luciérnaga Pale Ale. The fall seasonal La Parcela No. 1 Pumpkin Ale, introduced in 2008, finally ended confusion over why a brewery named Jolly Pumpkin didn't brew a pumpkin beer.

"Laurie and I had brainstormed a long list of names for the brewery, and we ended up choosing the most ridiculous one on the list because it kept making us laugh," said Jeffries. "Who names a brewery 'Jolly Pumpkin'?"

CHAPTER 12

"I'VE ALWAYS THOUGHT ANN ARBOR HAD A GREAT BEER SCENE"

In May 2013, Ann Arbor came in fourth out of twenty-three choices for "BeerCity USA" in homebrewing icon Charlie Papazian's annual poll. In its first year being included in the poll, Tree Town beat out Tampa, Florida, by a single vote but was more than twenty-six thousand votes shy of top vote-getter and BeerCity winner (for the second straight year) Grand Rapids.

It was a highly unscientific yet nonetheless encouraging sign that Ann Arbor's quiet contributions to Michigan's burgeoning craft beer movement were starting to be recognized. If slow and steady wins the race, the city is miles ahead.

"It's not just about the number of breweries, but about lifestyle and culture, about how you have to go out of your way *not* to find good beer," said Ashley's co-owner Roy More. "Virtually every bar or restaurant in central Ann Arbor has craft beer offerings."

"I've always thought Ann Arbor had a great beer scene," said Larry Bell, who still pays visits to his former town, including a February 2013 appearance to help celebrate the thirtieth anniversary of Ashley's. "We've had many, many years of great support for craft beer in Ann Arbor and Ypsilanti, especially since the Michigan Summer Beer Festival moved there."

One of Bell's newer beers, Quinannan Falls Special Lager, even had its genesis in a dream following a night out in Ann Arbor. "The idea for that beer came to me at the Campus Inn, after I left Ashley's and had late beers with some people in my hotel room," said Bell. "I was asleep barely twenty minutes when I woke up with this vivid dream of a waterfall in my head.

Onetime Ann Arbor resident Larry Bell joined Jeff More, daughter Laura Bell and Roy More to celebrate thirty years of Ashley's in February 2013. *Photo by Erik Smith.*

I knew the name of the beer and the full story of what it had to be. I even sketched the label art on the nightstand."

"Q Falls," as it's nicknamed, has "gotten a great response" among Bell's aficionados and beer lovers generally. It's so far available infrequently and on draft only, but Bell hopes that will eventually change. "The first time we brewed it, it was a home run out of the gate," he said. "But a dry-hopped lager? Talk about tying up your tanks. We haven't had a really good production run of the beer yet, but one of these days we will."

The beer and brewing scene in and around Ann Arbor, historically strong, only continues to grow. The past several years have witnessed many exciting new developments, and there's no sign that the tide of good beer flowing through Washtenaw County will ebb anytime soon.

In 2006, Matt and Rene Greff brought commercial brewing back to Ypsilanti when they opened the Corner Brewery, which produces and bottles nearly five thousand barrels of Arbor Brewing beers annually for distribution throughout the state. (Frog Island Brewing Company, a previous attempt to open a microbrewery by partners Dave French and Mike O'Brien, fizzled out when the cost became too high to bring the old grain mill property up to city code and zoning requirements. Frog Island

The recipe for Quinannan Falls Special Lager came to Larry Bell in a dream following a night out in Ann Arbor. *Bell's Brewery.*

beers, including Bengal IPA and Devil in the Details Imperial Stout, are contract brewed outside of Ypsilanti.)

Far more than a production facility, Corner has become a fixture in the life of the local community—exactly as the Greffs hoped it would.

"We've had so many people tell us, 'We don't know where we went before Corner.' There just wasn't a space like it," said Matt. "Our goal from day one was to create the sort of place we would want to hang out in, cross our fingers and hope others would enjoy it, too."

In the summer months, the Corner's enclosed beer garden brims with exhibits and performances from local artists, as well as relaxing music courtesy of area DJs at the Halcyon Sundaze series of events. Corner also hosts, in partnership with the Ann Arbor Brewers Guild, the annual Brews Crews, a homebrew competition that draws hundreds of entries from across Michigan and even from other states. And in the winter is Rat Fest, an event that showcases experimental beers brewed on the Corner's

"Rat Pad" small-batch system by homebrew clubs from throughout southeastern Michigan.

"These events help us continue to show our love for the homebrew community, which we came out of," said Matt.

That homebrew community got a big boost several years ago with the opening of the massive Adventures in Homebrewing store in a former beer and wine wholesaler warehouse on Ann Arbor's west side. It's a beer hobbyist's dream come true: a one-stop emporium with row after row of everything from starter kits to advanced kegging equipment and complete recipe kits based on popular styles or even specific commercial beers. Owners Jason Smith and Tyler Barber also fulfill and ship online orders all over the country, host demonstrations and events and, most importantly, provide advice and encouragement to veteran homebrewers and newbies alike.

Membership in the Ann Arbor Brewers Guild keeps climbing annually under the steady guidance of "benevolent dictator" Chris P. "Crispy" Frey. Michigan's oldest homebrew club boasts nearly 180 dues-paying home-grown beermakers of varying levels of ability, ensuring that the monthly meetings at members' homes remain a logistical nightmare. But no one seems inclined to change a thing about the way the club conducts its business.

Adventures in Homebrewing store owners Tyler Barber and Jason Smith with (left to right) Chris White and Kenzie Kuehnle (White Labs) and John Blichmann and Doug Granlund (Blichmann Engineering). *Photo by David Bardallis.*

"We're unusual in that we've never had officers or any formal management structure, so I'm often referred to by titles like 'chief anarchist,'" said Frey. "Someone always steps forward to take on chores and duties as needed, and we have a lot of fun along with a lot of good beer."

In late 2010, Ann Arbor welcomed Wolverine State Brewing Company, a brewery that was unusual in two ways. First, it wasn't located in a prime downtown location, but instead on the city's west side inside a former appliance store warehouse. And second, unlike almost every other microbrewery, the owners decided that it should specialize in lagers instead of ales.

"I grew up in Detroit, and Stroh's was all my dad drank," said co-owner Matt Roy. "I thought that that was something missing from the modern beer market in Michigan—just a good lager like Stroh's used to be. It was always more flavorful than Budweiser or Schlitz or Coors."

Following a few years of successful sales contracting with the now-defunct Michigan Brewing Company, Roy and his business partners, Trevor Thrall and E.T. Crowe, opened their production brewery and taproom on West Stadium Boulevard to immediate acclaim. Already they've expanded the brewhouse several times to meet on-premise demand and supply for distribution their four bottled beers: Wolverine Premium Lager, Wolverine Dark Lager, Wolverine Amber Lager and Gulo Gulo India Pale Lager. There are plans to bottle more varieties and continue to expand distribution throughout Michigan.

"We've banked on the notion that there's a real niche for lagers, that as people's beer palates get more and more sophisticated, the desire for complex, full-bodied lagers will catch on," said Roy. "Have we created something sustainable, or are we just keeping people occupied until the next thing comes along? Time will tell."

Jon Carlson and his partners have not been content to rest on their laurels. They continue to explore different bar and brewery concepts, expanding and enhancing the Ann Arbor beer scene with each new idea.

In 2008, they opened Blue Tractor BBQ and Brewery just down Washington Street from Grizzly Peak. "Our original concept with Blue Tractor was to offer retro-style, lighter American beers, which we felt would complement what was available at Grizzly Peak and at Arbor, for that matter. But we missed the mark there: Ann Arbor wanted the more flavorful brews."

After a few changes in brewers, Blue Tractor has achieved sustained success with Tim Schmidt in charge of the brewhouse. "We turned Tim loose and told him to make whatever was complex, crazy, weird," said Carlson. "Now we can't make enough beer, and the challenge ahead will be how to expand the brewery in that limited space."

"Chief anarchist" Chris Frey goes over new business at an Ann Arbor Brewers Guild meeting. *Photo by David Bardallis.*

Already Michigan's top-producing brewpub (more than 1,500 barrels annually) under longtime head brewer Duncan Williams, Grizzly Peak more than doubled its capacity in early 2013 when it replaced the original seven-barrel system with a fifteen-barrel one. (Fun fact: According to *Michigan Beer Guide*, the three Washington Street brewpubs—Grizzly, Blue Tractor and Arbor—together accounted for nearly 16 percent of the all the beer brewed in Michigan's forty-nine brewpubs in 2012.)

In July 2013, Carlson and company opened a new version of the townie-beloved Old German, which closed in 1995 after sixty-seven years when it was sold to make way for Grizzly Peak. The 2,400-square-foot basement bar underneath the brewpub pours out German-style beers directly from two large tanks and offers a limited menu of German-inspired snacks, including potato salad made from the original Old German's recipe.

"We just knew the Old German had to come back. Bud Metzger was a really nice guy, and I liked coming in to have lunch there," said Carlson. "Of course, it won't be like it was before. It will be more beer-focused."

Ron Jeffries joined forces with Carlson and his partners in 2008 to form Northern United Brewing Company, which owns the Jolly Pumpkin and North Peak beer brands. (Bottled Grizzly Peak beers will soon be distributed under the Northern United umbrella as well.) The partnership resulted in

Beer steins from Bud Metzger's original Old German restaurant. Jon Carlson and his partners recently revived the Old German in the basement beneath the Grizzly Peak brewpub. *From a December 1969 edition of the* Ann Arbor News. *All rights reserved. Reprinted with permission.*

the 2009 opening of the Jolly Pumpkin Café and Brewery on South Main Street, which serves Jolly Pumpkin and North Peak beers brewed by Jeffries in fifty- and sixty-barrel batches in Dexter. Limited Jolly Pumpkin releases, such as La Roja Grand Reserve, are available often only at the Ann Arbor café and typically sell out within hours.

Jeffries expects the spacious, seventy-thousand-square-foot Northern United brewery and headquarters, opened in early 2013, to enable him and his assistant brewers to expand production to twelve thousand barrels, with room to grow well beyond that. "When we moved the four hundred oak barrels of aging beer from the old Jolly Pumpkin brewery, I wondered how we ever even fit them all in that little space," he said. There are plans to eventually add a public taproom to the facility as well.

Brewing finally returned to Chelsea in 2013 nearly thirty years after Ted Badgerow closed the Real Ale Company. First came the January opening of Christopher Martinson's Chelsea Alehouse Brewery, followed in the summer by Bitter Old Fecker Rustic Ales, a nanobrewery started by former Grizzly Peak assistant brewer Nathan Hukill that periodically produces small batches of barrel-aged beers.

Other signs of the vibrant and growing local beer culture continue to pop up everywhere in Ann Arbor. Hannah Cheadle and Walt Hansen, owners of artisan sausage and jerky makers Biercamp, added a one-barrel system to their South State Street shop and offer growler fills from rotating taps of Pale Ale, Smoked Porter, Brown Ale, Wheat Ale and "flagship" Vienna IPA. Mark Hodesh and retired school principal Bill Zolkowski collaborated to create Bill's Beer Garden, a part-time European-style drinking spot that operates during the off-hours in the well-appointed parking lot of Hodesh's Downtown Home and Garden. A new forty-tap craft beer bar opened on South University, in the midst of the cheap swill–drinking student population. And many area restaurants, like the farm-to-table Grange Kitchen and Bar on West Liberty Street, not only pour great beer but also routinely host beer dinners, carefully pairing courses of dishes made from locally sourced ingredients with Michigan-produced brews.

Chef Brandon Johns of Grange Kitchen & Bar hosts regular beer dinners at his downtown Ann Arbor restaurant. *Photo by David Bardallis.*

"The craft beer scene goes hand in hand with what we're all about—fresh and local. Our beer dinners have been amazingly popular, and they almost always sell out early," said owner and chef Brandon Johns. "We're really lucky to have so many great breweries here. There's enough good beer of every style in Michigan that you never get tired or bored with any of it."

Longtime Ann Arbor institutions like Fraser's Pub are also looking forward to a bright beer future even as they celebrate historical milestones. Fraser's, once the exclusive domain of beers such as late founder Red Fraser's favorite, Schlitz, has, under the ownership of Ron Sartori, become a craft brew destination. The townie hangout has more than doubled its number of taps to twenty and even serves cask ale now; sales have never been better. For the pub's fiftieth anniversary bash in 2012, Sartori commissioned Arbor Brewing to create a special imperial rye IPA as part of the celebration.

And Ann Arbor's German heritage continues strongly into its third century of proud beer-centric culture. Since its founding in the 1930s, the German Park Club has hosted annual summer picnics full of traditional food, music, dancing and, of course, beer. For decades, these events, held on the club's park grounds on Pontiac Trail north of town, were something of a secret among Ann Arborites "in the know." But they have exploded in

The neighborhood pub founded by Red Fraser and run by his family for more than four decades is now a booming Ann Arbor craft beer destination. *Peter Yates, for the June 1981 edition of the* Ann Arbor Observer.

popularity in recent years, thanks to the increasing number of seekers after beer culture and tradition, as well as Internet word of mouth. In 2013, the German Park Club turned seventy-five years old and commemorated the occasion, appropriately enough, with a big October beer gala.

Of course, no one can say for sure what the present-day beer boom means for the long-term future of brew in the city, nor is there any crystal ball to determine what the magical "saturation point" in the local beer-drinking market might be. But if Shakespeare is correct that the past is prologue, Ann Arbor's rich brewing history would seem to ensure that we will remain a lively and proud beer-loving town until roughly sometime between when the cows come home and the stars turn cold.

I'll drink to that.

THE GUIDE TO GOOD BEER IN ANN ARBOR AND BEYOND

BREWPUBS

Arbor Brewing Company
114 East Washington Street, Ann Arbor, MI 48104
Established: 1995
(734) 213-1393
www.arborbrewing.com/pub

Blue Tractor BBQ & Brewery
207 East Washington Street, Ann Arbor, MI 48104
Established: 2008
(734) 222-4095
www.bluetractor.net/bta/a2/index

Grizzly Peak Brewing Company
120 West Washington Street, Ann Arbor, MI 48104
Established: 1995
(734) 741-7325
www.grizzlypeak.net

MICROBREWERIES

Biercamp
1643 South State Street, Ann Arbor, MI 48104
Established: 2011
(734) 995-BIER (2437)
www.bier-camp.com

Bitter Old Fecker Rustic Ales
12855 Old U.S. 12 Highway East, Chelsea, MI 48118
Established: 2013
Production only—no public taproom
(734) 444-5201
www.facebook.com/pages/Bitter-Old-Fecker-Rustic-Ales/131864156886996

Chelsea Alehouse Brewery
420 North Main Street, Suite 100, Chelsea, MI 48118
Established: 2013
(734) 433-5500
www.chelseaalehouse.com

Corner Brewery
720 Norris Street, Ypsilanti, MI 48198
Established: 2006
(734) 480-2739
www.cornerbrewery.com

Jolly Pumpkin Café & Brewery
311 South Main Street, Ann Arbor, MI 48104
Established: 2009
(734) 913-2730
www.jollypumpkin.com/annarbor/Default.htm

Liberty Street Brewing Company
149 West Liberty Street, Plymouth, MI 48170
Established: 2008
(734) 207-9600
www.libertystreetbeer.com

Northern United Brewing Company
2319 Bishop Circle East, Dexter, MI 48130
Established: 2004
Production brewery for Jolly Pumpkin Artisan Ales and North Peak Brewing
  Company
(734) 426-4962
www.nubco.net

Original Gravity Brewing Company
440 County Street, Milan, MI 48160
Established: 2008
(734) 439-7490
www.ogbrewing.com

Unity Vibration
93 Ecorse Road, Ypsilanti, MI 48198
Established: 2008
(734) 277-4063
www.unityvibrationkombucha.com

Witch's Hat Brewing Company
22235 Pontiac Trail, South Lyon, MI 48178
Established: 2011
(248) 486-2595
www.witchshatbrewing.com

Wolverine State Brewing Company
2019 West Stadium Boulevard, Ann Arbor, MI 48103
Established: 2010
(734) 369-2990
www.wolverinebeer.com

PUBS

Ashley's
338 South State Street, Ann Arbor, MI 48104
Established: 1983
(734) 996-9191
www.ashleys.com

Bill's Beer Garden
218 South Ashley Street, Ann Arbor, MI 48104
Established: 2012
(734) 369-8001
www.billsbeergarden.com

Dan's Downtown Tavern
103 East Michigan Avenue, Saline, MI 48176
Established: 1997
(734) 429-3159
www.facebook.com/DANSBARS

Dominick's
812 Monroe Street, Ann Arbor, MI 48104
Established: 1960
(734) 662-5414

Fraser's Pub
2045 Packard Street, Ann Arbor, MI 48104
Established: 1962
(734) 665-1955
www.fraserspubaa.com

Heidelberg
215 North Main Street, Ann Arbor, MI 48104
Established: 1961
(734) 663-7758
www.heidelbergannarbor.com

Jet's Pizza Sportsroom
506 North Main Street, Chelsea, MI 48118
(734) 433-9700

Old Town Tavern
122 West Liberty Street, Ann Arbor, MI 48104
Established: 1972
(734) 662-9291
www.oldtownaa.com

The Shark Club
1140 Pinckney Road, Howell, MI 48843
Established: 2007
(517) 540-0300
www.sharkclubhowell.com

Sidetrack Bar & Grill
56 East Cross Street, Ypsilanti, MI 48198
Established: 1979
(734) 483-1490
www.sidetrackbarandgrill.com

World of Beer
1300 South University Avenue, Ann Arbor, MI 48104
Established: 2013
(734) 913-2430
www.wobusa.com/Locations/AnnArbor.aspx

The Wurst Bar
705 West Cross Street, Ypsilanti, MI 48197
Established: 2012
(734) 485-6720
www.wurstbarypsi.com

Restaurants

Grange Kitchen & Bar
118 West Liberty Street, Ann Arbor, MI 48103
Established: 2009
(734) 995-2107
www.grangekitchenandbar.com

Metzger's
305 North Zeeb Road, Ann Arbor MI 48103
Established: 1928
(734) 668-8987
www.metzgers.net

Red Rock Downtown Barbecue
207 West Michigan Avenue, Ypsilanti, MI 48197
Established: 2012
(734) 340-2381
www.redrockypsi.com

Terry B's Restaurant & Bar
7954 Ann Arbor Street, Dexter, MI 48130
Established: 2006
(734) 426-3727
www.terrybs.com

Retail

A&L Wine Castle
2424 West Stadium Boulevard, Ann Arbor, MI 48103
Hours: Monday–Thursday, 9:00 a.m.–10:00 p.m.; Friday–Saturday, 9:00 a.m.–
    11:00 p.m.; Sunday, noon–9:00 p.m.
(734) 665-WINE (9463)
www.aandlwinecastle.com

Arbor Farms Market
2103 West Stadium Boulevard, Ann Arbor, MI 48103
Hours: 8:00 a.m.–9:00 p.m. every day
(734) 996-8111
www.arborfarms.com

The Beer Depot
114 East William Street, Ann Arbor, MI 48104
Hours: 7:00 a.m.–2:00 a.m. every day

(734) 623-4430
www.annarborbeerdepot.com

Hiller's Market
3615 Washtenaw Avenue, Ann Arbor, MI 48104
Hours: Monday–Saturday, 8:00 a.m.–10:00 p.m.; Sunday, 8:00 a.m.–9:00 p.m.
(734) 677-2370
www.hillers.com

Main Street Party Store
201 North Main Street, Ann Arbor, MI 48104
Hours: Monday–Friday, 7:00 a.m.–2:00 a.m.; Saturday, 8:00 a.m.–2:00 a.m.;
    Sunday, 11:00 a.m.–2:00 a.m.
(734) 769-1515
www.mainwine.com

MI General Store
44 East Cross Street, Ypsilanti, MI 48198
Hours: Tuesday–Saturday, 10:00 a.m.–7:00 p.m.; Sunday, noon–7:00 p.m.
(734) 961-8039
www.facebook.com/pages/MI-General-Store/251075844924825

Plum Market
375 North Maple Road, Ann Arbor, MI 48103
Hours: 8:00 a.m.–10:00 p.m. every day
(734) 827-5000
blog.plummarket.com/plum-market-ann-arbor

Whole Foods Market Cranbrook
990 West Eisenhower Parkway, Ann Arbor, MI 48103
Hours: 8:00 a.m.–10:00 p.m. every day
(734) 997-7500
www.wholefoodsmarket.com/stores/cranbrook

The Wine Seller
2721 Plymouth Road, Ann Arbor, MI 48105
Hours: Monday–Saturday, 10:00 a.m.–9:00 p.m.; Sunday, noon–6:00 p.m.
(734) 668-8086
www.aawineseller.com

FESTIVALS AND EVENTS

Brews Crews Homebrew Competition
720 Norris Street, Ypsilanti, MI 48198
brewscrews.aabg.org
When: Annually in June

German Park Picnic
5549 Pontiac Trail, Ann Arbor, MI 48105
www.germanpark.com
When: Last Saturday of June, July and August

Michigan Brewers Guild Summer Beer Festival
Riverside Park, Ypsilanti, MI
www.mbgmash.org/beer-fest-101/sbf
When: Annually in July

Rat Fest
720 Norris Street, Ypsilanti, MI 48198
http://www.arborbrewing.com/rat
When: Annually in January

HOMEBREWING

Adventures in Homebrewing
6071 Jackson Road, Ann Arbor, MI 48103
Hours: Monday–Friday, 10:00 a.m.–7:00 p.m.; Saturday, 10:00 a.m.–5:00 p.m.;
   Sunday, noon–4:00 p.m.
(313) 277-BREW
www.homebrewing.org

Ann Arbor Brewers Guild
www.aabg.org
info@aabg.org
Meets monthly at rotating members' homes

The Beer Depot
Also sells homebrewing supplies; see entry under "Retail"

Sons of Liberty Homebrew Club
www.solhbc.org
info@solhbc.org
Meets first Monday of the month at Liberty Street Brewing Company or a
   member's home

South Lyon Area Brewers
www.facebook.com/pages/South-Lyon-Area-Brewers/357776834284980
Meets monthly at Witch's Hat Brewing Company

BIBLIOGRAPHY

BOOKS

Arnold, John P., and Frank Penman. *History of the Brewing Industry and Brewing Science in America*. Cleveland, OH: BeerBooks.com, 2006. Originally published in 1933.

Beakes, Samuel W. *Past and Present of Washtenaw County, Michigan: Together with Biographical Sketches of Many of Its Prominent and Leading Citizens and Illustrious Dead*. Chicago, IL: S.J. Clarke Publishing Company, 1906.

Bien, Laura. *Tales from the Ypsilanti Archives*. Charleston, SC: The History Press, 2010.

Blum, Peter H. *Brewed in Detroit: Breweries and Beers Since 1830*. Detroit, MI: Wayne State University Press, 1999.

Chase, A.W. *Dr. Chase's Recipes, or, Information for Everybody....* Ann Arbor, MI, 1865.

Finney, Byron Alfred, ed. *A Third Volume Devoted to Washtenaw County*. Dayton, OH: National Historical Association, 1924.

Harburg, Ernie. *Liberty, Equality, Consensus, and All That Jazz at the Del Rio Bar*. Ann Arbor, MI: Huron River Press, 2009.

History of Washtenaw County, Michigan: Together with Sketches of Its Cities, Villages and Townships... and Biographies of Representative Citizens. Chicago, IL: Charles C. Chapman & Co., 1881.

Logghe, Michael. *True Crimes and the History of the Ann Arbor Police Department*. N.p., 2002. Accessed at aapd.aadl.org/aapd/truecrimes.

Love, Edmund G. *Hanging On: Or How to Get Through a Depression and Enjoy Life*. New York: William Morrow and Company, 1972.

Mann, James Thomas. *Wicked Ann Arbor*. Charleston, SC: The History Press, 2011.

Miller, Charles H. *Auden: An American Friendship*. New York: Paragon House, 1989.

Nation, Carrie. *The Use and Need of the Life of Carry A. Nation*. Topeka, KS: F.M. Steves & Sons, 1905.

Ogle, Maureen. *Ambitious Brew: The Story of American Beer*. Orlando, FL, Harcourt, 2006.

Okrent, Daniel. *Last Call: The Rise and Fall of Prohibition*. New York: Scribner, 2010.

Peckham, Howard Henry. *The Making of the University of Michigan: 1817–1992.* Ann Arbor: University of Michigan Bentley Historical Library, 1997.

Reade, Marjorie, and Susan Wineberg. *Historic Buildings, Ann Arbor, Michigan.* Ann Arbor, MI: Ann Arbor Historic District Commission, 1992.

Smith, Gregg. *Beer in America: The Early Years 1587–1840.* Boulder, CO: Siris Books, 1998.

Stephenson, Orlando W. *Ann Arbor: The First Hundred Years.* Ann Arbor, MI: Ann Arbor Chamber of Commerce, 1927.

Stevens, Wystan, ed. *Northfield Harvest: A Pictorial History of Northfield Township and the Whitmore Lake Area.* Whitmore Lake, MI: Northfield Township Historical Society, 1999.

Szymanski, Ann-Marie E. *Pathways to Prohibition: Radicals, Moderates, and Social Movement Outcomes.* Durham, NC: Duke University Press, 2003.

NEWSPAPER, MAGAZINE AND ONLINE ARTICLES

Ann Arbor Daily News. "Noisy Crowds Receive Brew." April 7, 1933.

[Ann Arbor] *Daily Times News.* "Have You a Little Brewery at Home?" June 2, 1919.

———. "Rum Runners Taken After Wild Chase." June 2, 1919.

Ann Arbor Sun. "Interview with Commander Cody: Hometown Boy Makes Good." May 31, 1974.

Ann Arbor Times News. "Officers Arrest 6 Over Week-End." December 11, 1922.

———. "State Officers Make a Cleanup." December 23, 1921.

Asimov, Eric. "A Delicious Free for All." *New York Times*, February 24, 2010. nytimes.com/2010/02/24/dining/reviews/24wine.html.

Bangs, Lester. "Iggy Pop: Blowtorch in Bondage." *Village Voice*, March 28, 1977.

Beberman, Mallory. "A True Divide: A Look Back at Campus During the Prohibition Era." *Michigan Daily*, November 2, 2010. michigandaily.com/content/prohibition-era-ann-arbor.

Chang, Kenneth. "Donald Glaser, Nobel Winner in Physics, Dies at 86." *New York Times*, March 4, 2013. nytimes.com/2013/03/05/science/donald-glaser-nobel-winner-in-physics-dies-at-86.html.

Chapman, Robert L. "Auden in Ann Arbor." *Michigan Quarterly Review* (Fall 1978).

Dix, Jennifer. "Ann Arborites: Flame Bartender Harry Tselios." *Ann Arbor Observer*, April 1989.

Dooley, Greg, "Snow Generates a Fever and a Thirst." MVictors.com, November 8, 2012. mvictors.com/?p=34193.

Engelmann, Larry. "Old Saloon Days in Michigan." *Michigan History* (Summer 1977).

Erlewine, Michael. "Schwaben Inn, 215 S. Ashley Street." ArborWiki. arborwiki.org/Schwaben_Inn.

Frank, Mary Jane. "Drug Abuse Appears on Decline Here." *Ann Arbor News*, December 9, 1973. oldnews.aadl.org/node/72529.

Fraser, Kelly. "A Legacy of Students and Beer." *Michigan Daily*, January 25, 2008. michigandaily.com/content/legacy-students-and-beer.

Glaser, Donald A. "Banquet Speech." Nobelprize.org, December 10, 1960. nobelprize.org/nobel_prizes/physics/laureates/1960/glaser-speech.html.

Glenn, Alan. "The Doors' Disaster at Michigan." *Michigan Today*, November 10, 2010. michigantoday.umich.edu/2010/11/story.php?id=7894.

Gould, Mike. "A Barn Dance with Bob Seger." *Ann Arbor Observer*, March 2007. mondodyne.com/a2observer/segerbarndance.shtml.

Hunt, Mary. "Beer the Way Ann Arbor Liked It." *Ann Arbor News*, March 16, 1975. oldnews.aadl.org/aa_news_19750316_p15-beer_the_way_ann_arbor_liked_it.

Kerwin, Fred, and Marjorie Kerwin. "Dr. Chase's Wonderful Book." *Ann Arbor Observer*, October 1980.

LeLievre, Roger. "Leopold Bros. Keeps Evolving." *Ann Arbor News*, November 4, 2004.

Mann, James Thomas. "Distillery Found on the Widow Gotts Farm." Ypsihistor, January 4, 2010. ypsihistor.blogspot.com/2010/01/distillery-found-on-widow-gotts-farm.html.

———. "Students Arrested with Beer." Ypsihistor, February 7, 2013. ypsihistor. blogspot.com/2013/02/students-arrested-with-beer.html.

Murawski, Margaret. "Historic Houses." *Huron Valley Ad-Visor*, October 16, 1968. oldnews.aadl.org/node/80361.

Nash, Kevin. "Monroe Man Opened First Brewery in Ypsilanti." BlogsMonroe, February 14, 2009. blogsmonroe.com/beer/2009/02/monroe-man-opened-first-brewery-in-ypsilanti.

Owosso Argus-Press. "High Court Knocks Out Law Forbidding Drinking of Liquor." February 19, 1919.

Papazian, Charlie. "Grand Rapids, Michigan Is BeerCity USA 2013." Examiner.com, May 13, 2013. examiner.com/article/grand-rapids-michigan-is-beercity-usa-2013.

Pattison, Charles Rich. "Ypsilanti: Its Past, Present, and Future" (Part II). *Ypsilanti Commercial*, May 23, 1874, as posted at ypsigleanings.aadl.org/ypsigleanings/13478.

Phillips, Marcia. "Lost Ypsilanti—The Malt House." Ypsilanti Historical Society. ypsilantihistoricalsociety.org/publications/malthouse.html.

Shackman, Grace. "Brewed on Fourth Street." *Ann Arbor Observer*, December 2007. aaobserver.aadl.org/aaobserver/18545.

———. "The Court Tavern." *Ann Arbor Observer*, January 1996. aaobserver.aadl. org/aaobserver/17689.

———. "Dr. Chase's Successors." *Ann Arbor Observer*, November 1993. aaobserver. aadl.org/aaobserver/17605.

———. "439 Fifth Street: From Drinking Spot to Play Yard." *Ann Arbor Observer*, January 1992. aaobserver.aadl.org/aaobserver/15423.

———. "The Germans in Ann Arbor." *Ann Arbor Observer*, August 2001. aaobserver. aadl.org/aaobserver/18385.

The Smoking Gun. "Iggy Pop and the Stooges and the Seven Dwarfs." September 28, 2012. thesmokinggun.com/documents/iggy-pop-rider-798451.

Stevenson, Anne. "When the Kissing Had to Stop: Remembering the University of Michigan in the 1950s." *Michigan Quarterly Review* (Spring 2003). hdl.handle. net/2027/spo.act2080.0042.216.

Stevens, Wystan. "Ann Arbor Brewing Co.: A Brewery Off Broadway." *Huron Valley Ad-Visor*, April 18, 1973. oldnews.aadl.org/node/80459.

Time. "Small Is Tasty." July 25, 1983.

Tobin, James. "Car Craze." *Michigan Today*, February 9, 2011. michigantoday.umich. edu/2011/02/story.php?id=7934.

———. "Earth Day Eve." *Michigan Today*, March 10, 2010. michigantoday.umich. edu/2010/03/story.php?id=7629.

———. "The Great Raid." *Michigan Today*, June 10, 2009. michigantoday.umich. edu/2009/06/story.php?id=7489.

Treml, William B. "Drug Traffic, Arrests Brisk Here." *Ann Arbor News*, March 3, 1969. oldnews.aadl.org/node/72350.

Walter P. Reuther Library blog, Wayne State University. "The Windsor-Detroit Funnel: Prohibition in Detroit." January 17, 2012. reuther.wayne.edu/node/8334.

Wieland, George F. "Beloved Beer: Germans, Yankees, and Prohibition." *Ann Arbor Observer*, September 2009. arborweb.com/articles/beloved_beer_full_article.html.

EXHIBITS, DOCUMENTS, SPEECHES AND WHITE PAPERS

Bad Habits: Drinks, Drags and Drugs in Washtenaw County History. Washtenaw County Historical Society exhibit, April 2012. washtenawhistory.org.

Foote, Henry Wilder. "The Saloon in Ann Arbor." Ann Arbor, MI, 1909. Accessed at catalog.hathitrust.org/Record/003935806.

"A Special Message of Governor Chase S. Osborn to the Forty-sixth Legislature of the State of Michigan in Extraordinary Session." March 11, 1912. Accessed at books.google.com/books?id=PEjiAAAAMAAJ.

Taylor, John C. "Michigan's Liquor Distribution Systems: An Historical Review and Analysis." Paper presented at CHARM (Conference on Historical Analysis and Research in Marketing). Available at http://faculty.quinnipiac.edu/charm. Wayne State University, Detroit, MI, 1992.

INTERVIEWS

The following people were interviewed—in person, by phone or via e-mail—specifically for this book: Ted Badgerow, Larry Bell, Jon Carlson, Max Cope, Karl Dickinson, Chris P. "Crispy" Frey, Marc Grasso, Matt and Rene Greff, Mark Hodesh, Ron and Laurie Jeffries, Brandon Johns, Todd Leopold, Roy More, John Pruder, Jim Rees, Jeff Renner, Norm Richert, Matt Roy, Ron Sartori, Barry Seifer, Doug Smith, Wystan Stevens, Jim Wanty, Robert Jr Whitall and Bill Zolkowski.

WEBSITES

Ann Arbor City Council minutes. councilminutes.aadl.org. Searchable archive of city council minutes from 1891 to 1930.

Ann Arbor District Library Old News. oldnews.aadl.org. Searchable archive of images and articles from historical newspapers, including the *Ann Arbor Courier*, *Ann Arbor Argus*, *Ann Arbor Sun*, *Ann Arbor Observer* and *Ann Arbor News*.

Ann Arbor Observer. "Then & Now." aaobserver.aadl.org. Collection of local history articles published in the *Observer* over the past three decades.

ArborWiki. arborwiki.org. Collaborative, community-driven effort to share local knowledge about the Ann Arbor area.

Brewers Association. brewersassociation.org.

Michigan Beer Guide. michiganbeerguide.com.

Ypsilanti Gleanings. ypsigleanings.aadl.org. Archive of articles from the official publication of the Ypsilanti Historical Society.

INDEX

ABOUT THE AUTHOR

David Bardallis writes regular beer columns for annarbor. com and *Great Lakes Brewing News* and is a frequent contributor to *Michigan Beer Guide*. A lifelong Michigander, longtime craft beer drinker and occasional homebrewer, he lives in Ann Arbor, where he works as a freelance writer and editor when not visiting the local bars and breweries. More of his beer writing can be found at his blog, annarborbeer.com, and on mittenbrew.com. Follow him on Facebook at "All the Brews Fit to Pint" or Twitter at @allthebrews.